THE BEST OF ADULT COLORING BOOKS BY PRESTON

VOLUME ONE

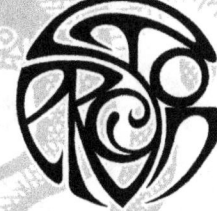

ISBN 978-1-387-46729-7

The collection of illustrations in this book comes from:
CRITTERS, CREATURES & CUTIES
DEN'S DOODLES (Regular & Captionated)
DEN'S DOODLES - 2fers
PRESTON POTPOURRI Volume One
PRESTON POTPOURRI Volume Two

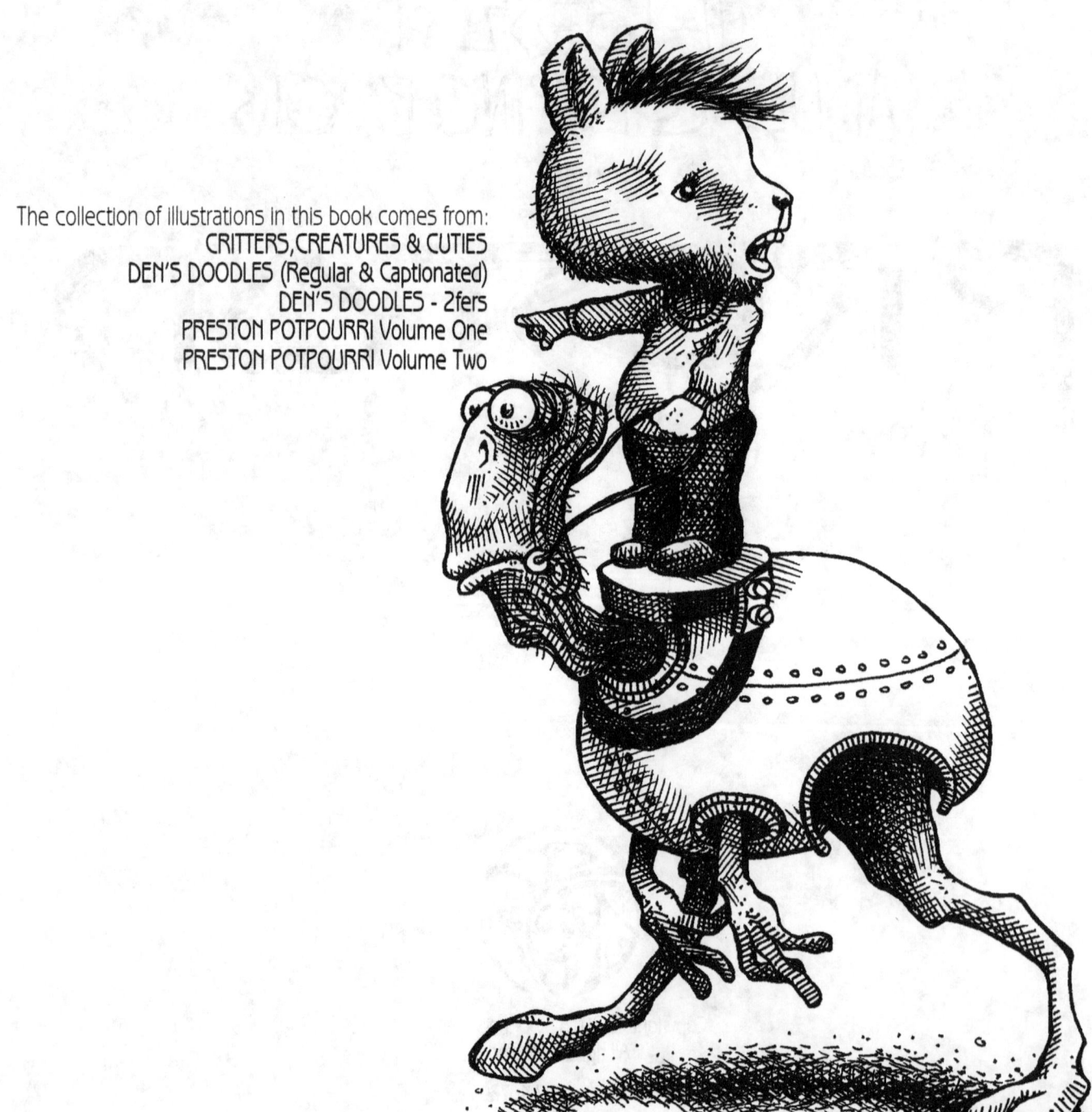

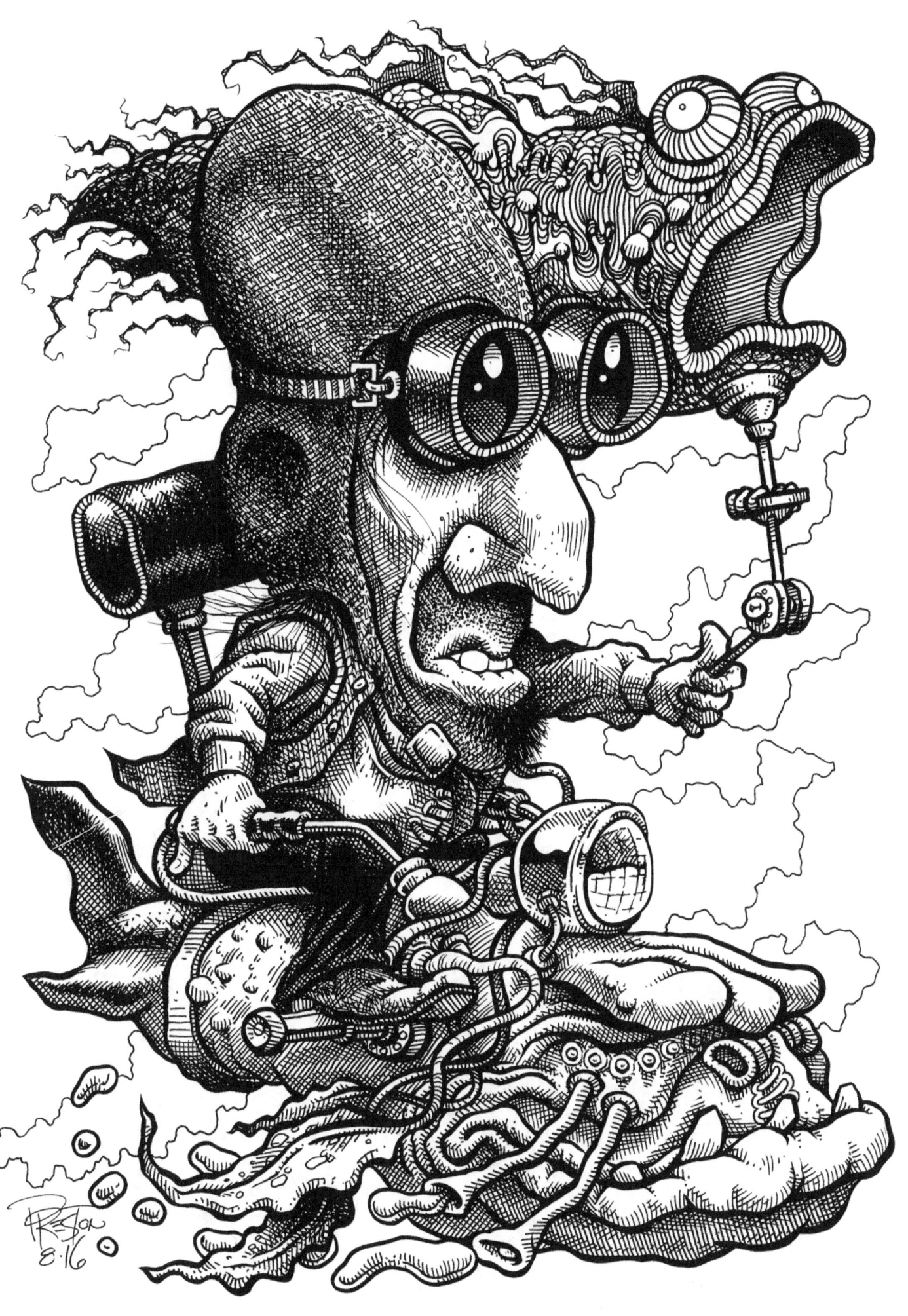

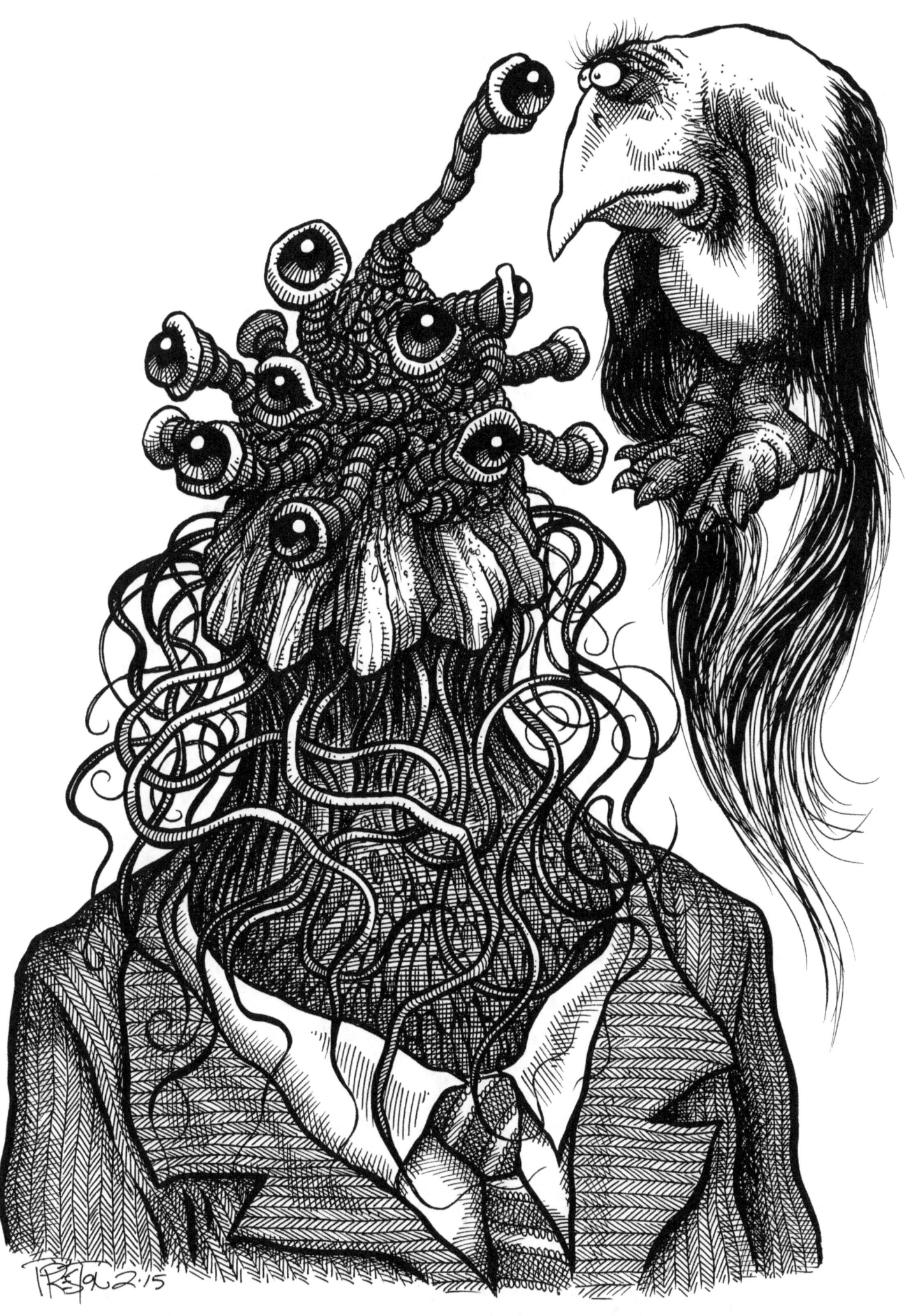

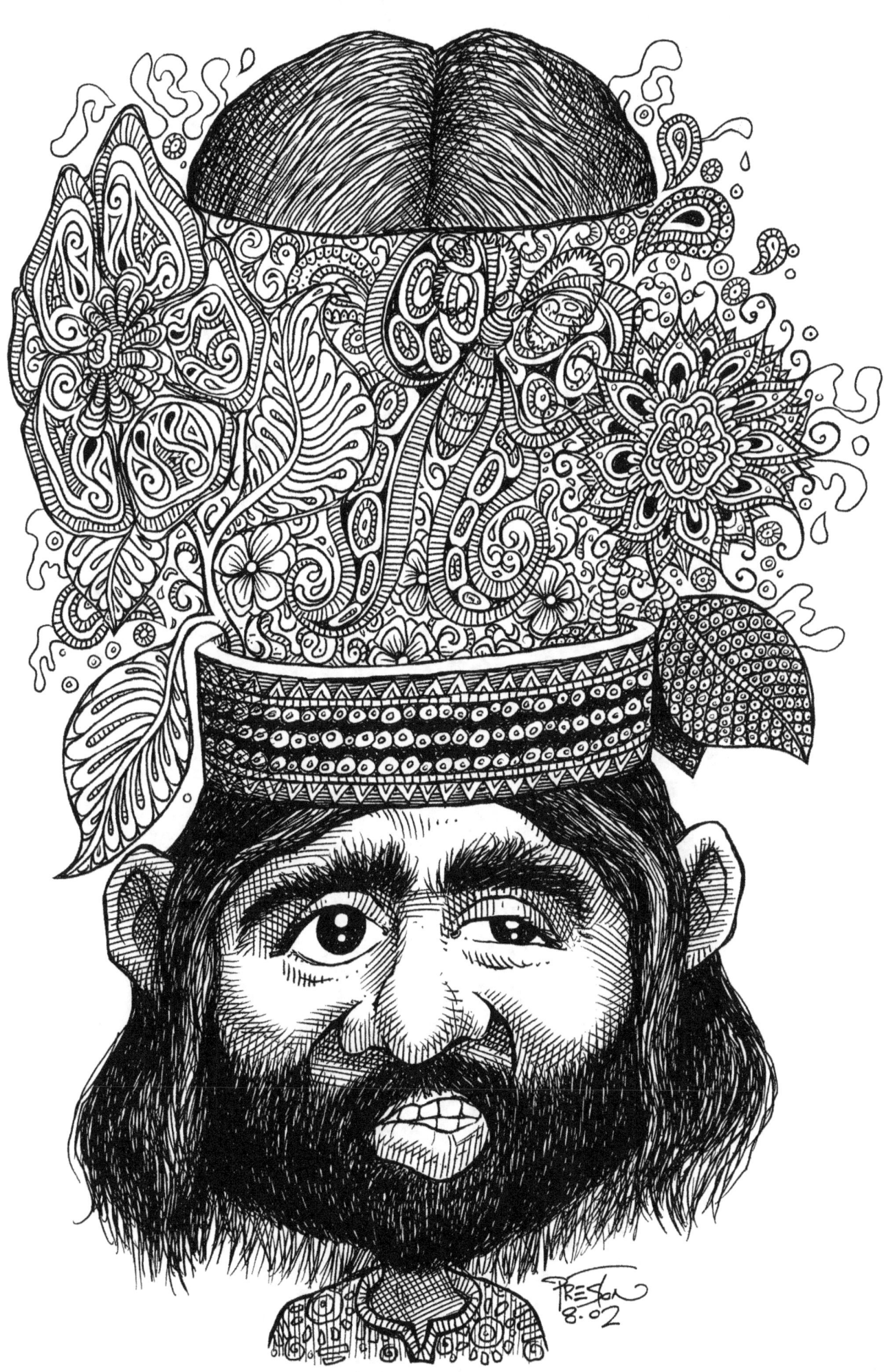

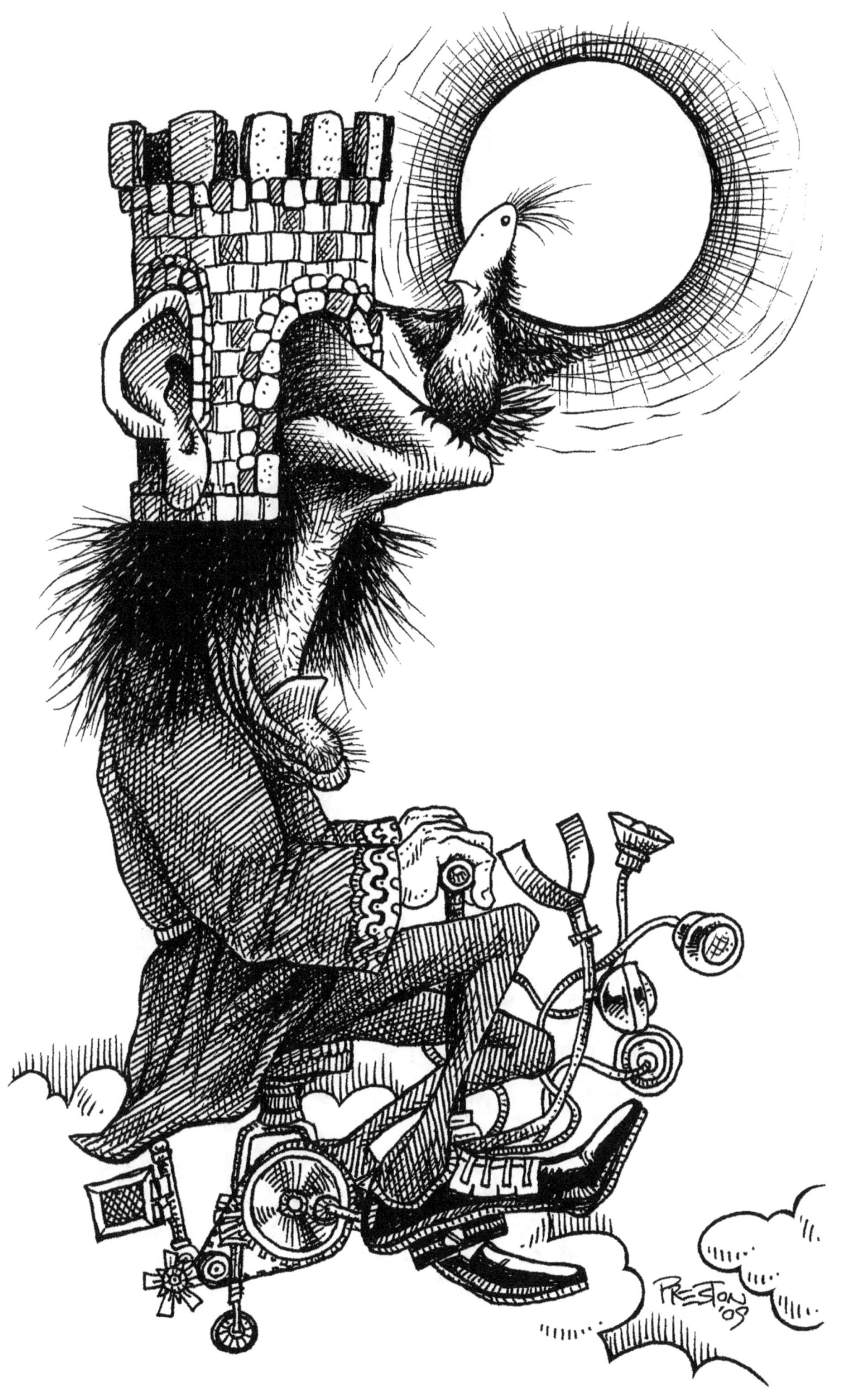

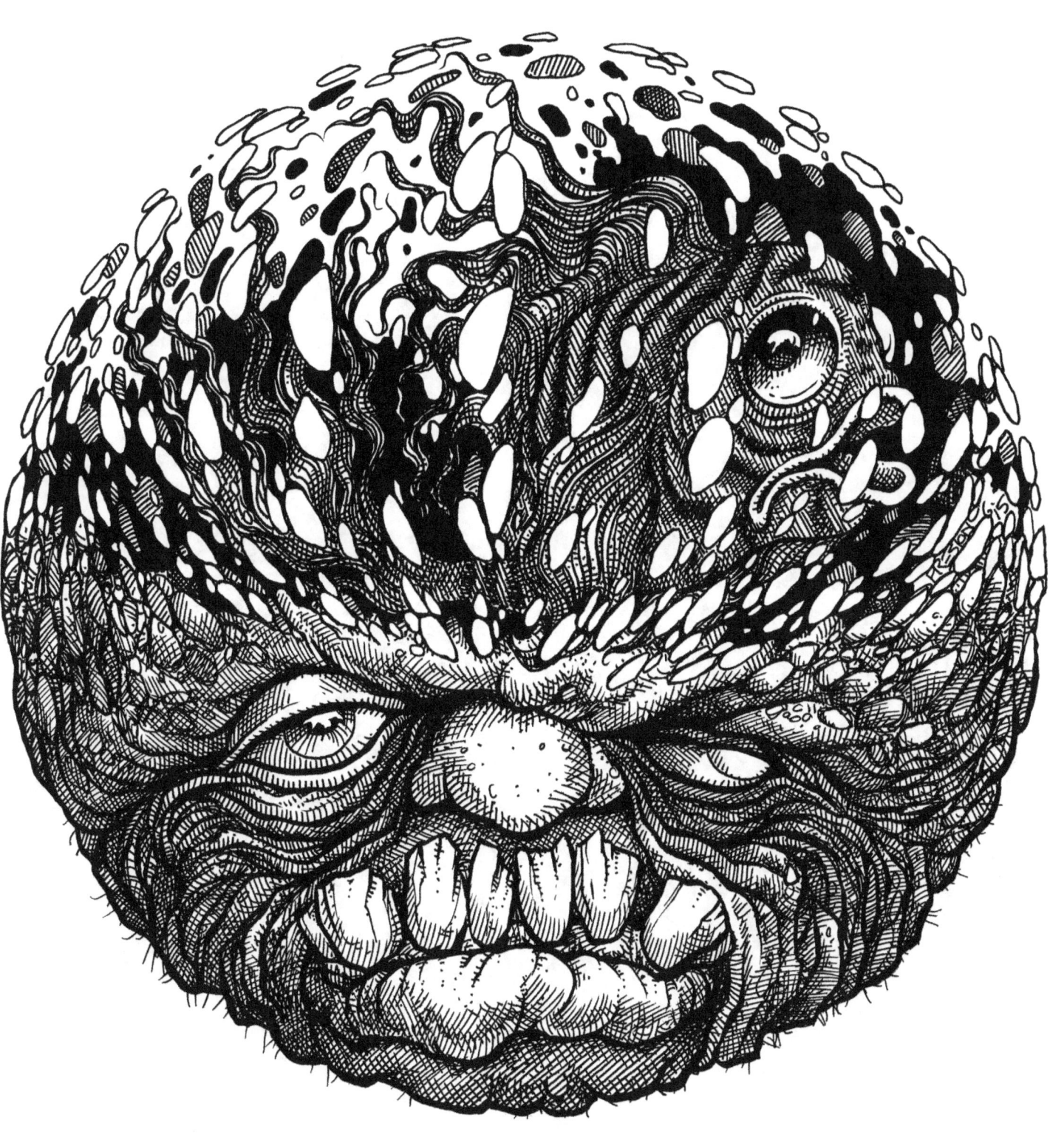

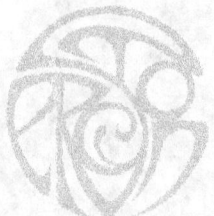

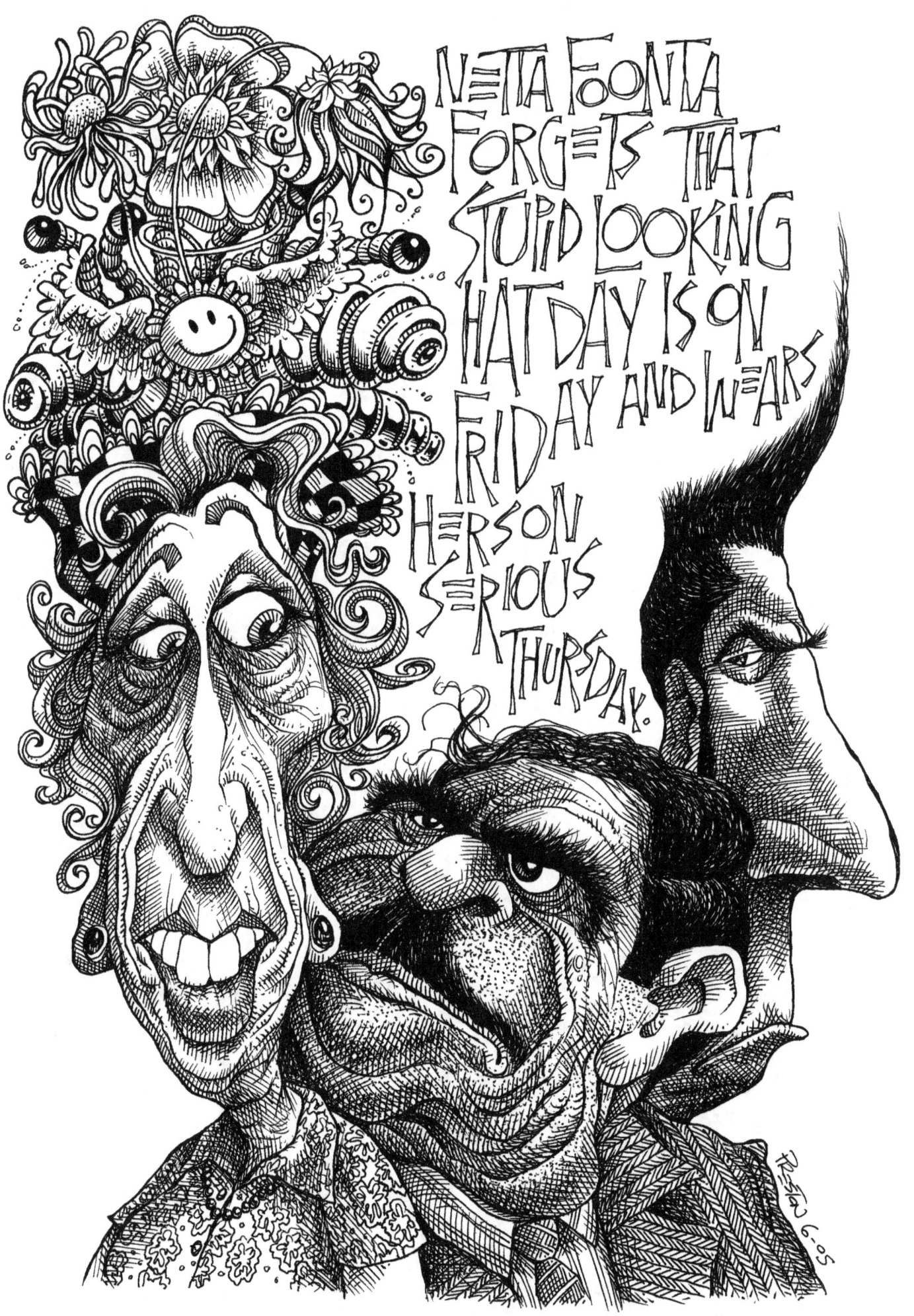

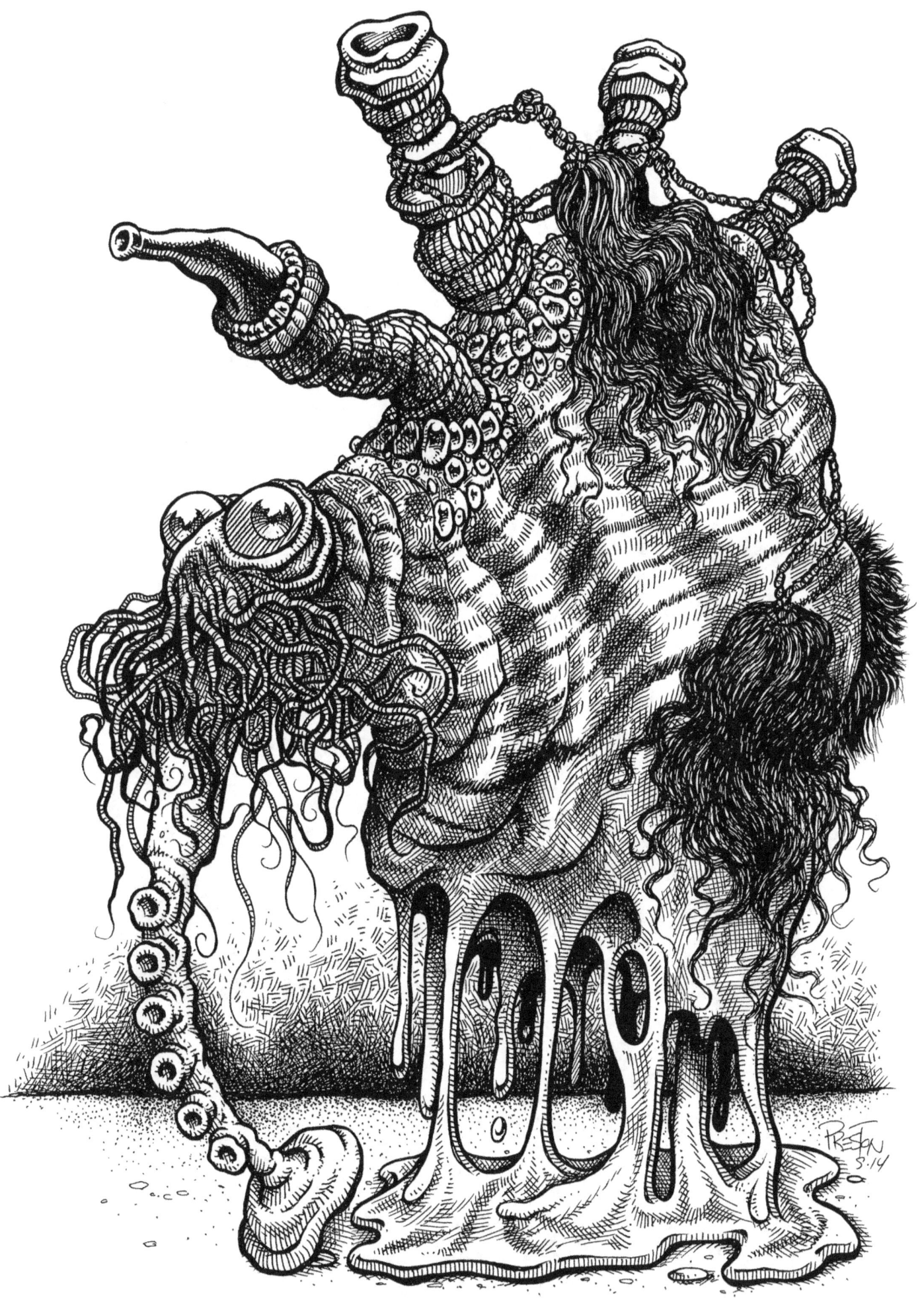

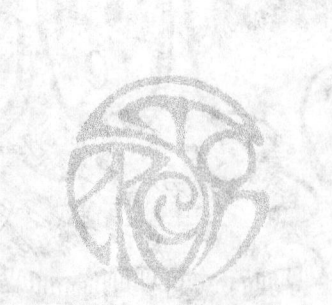

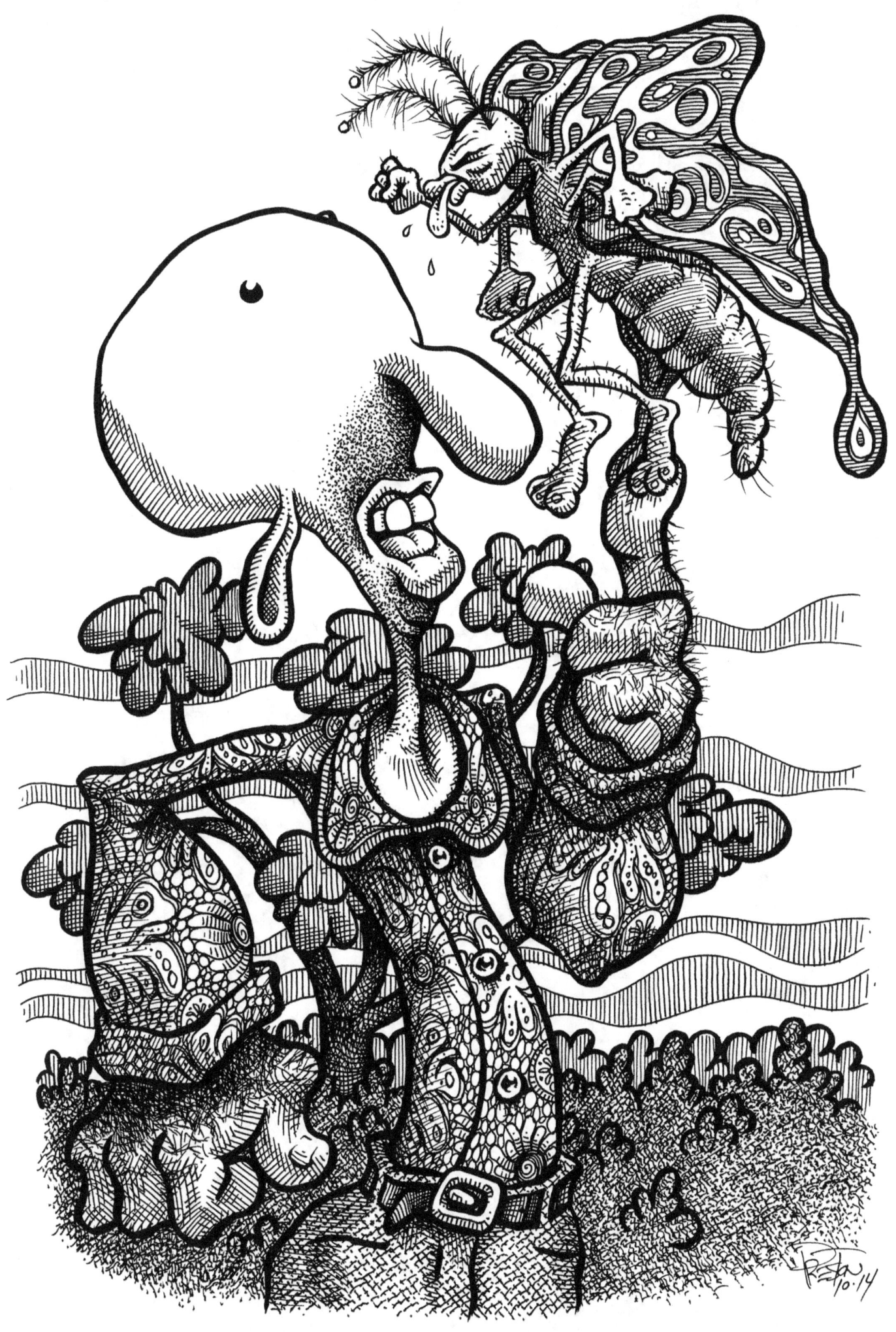

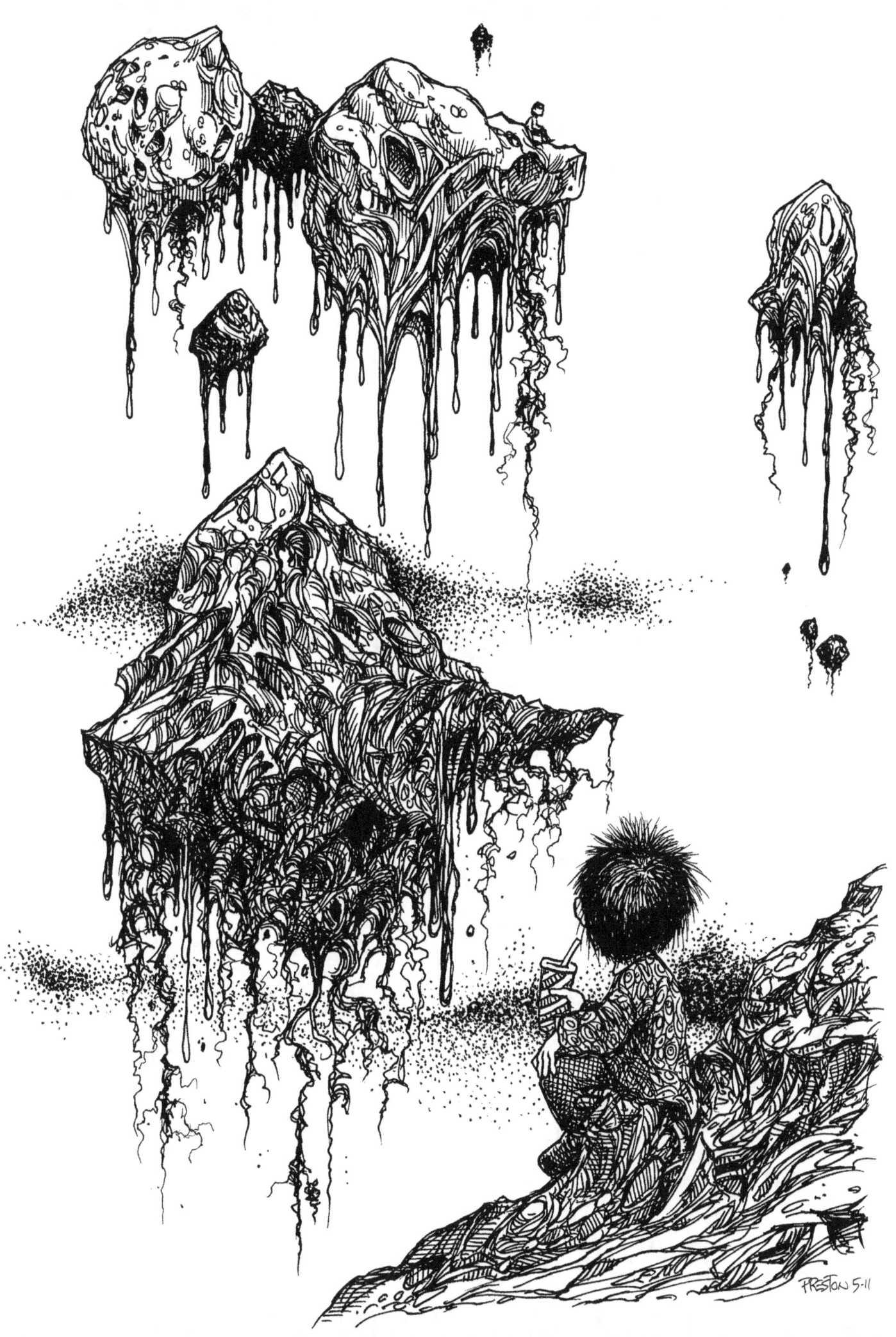

PRESTON 5-11

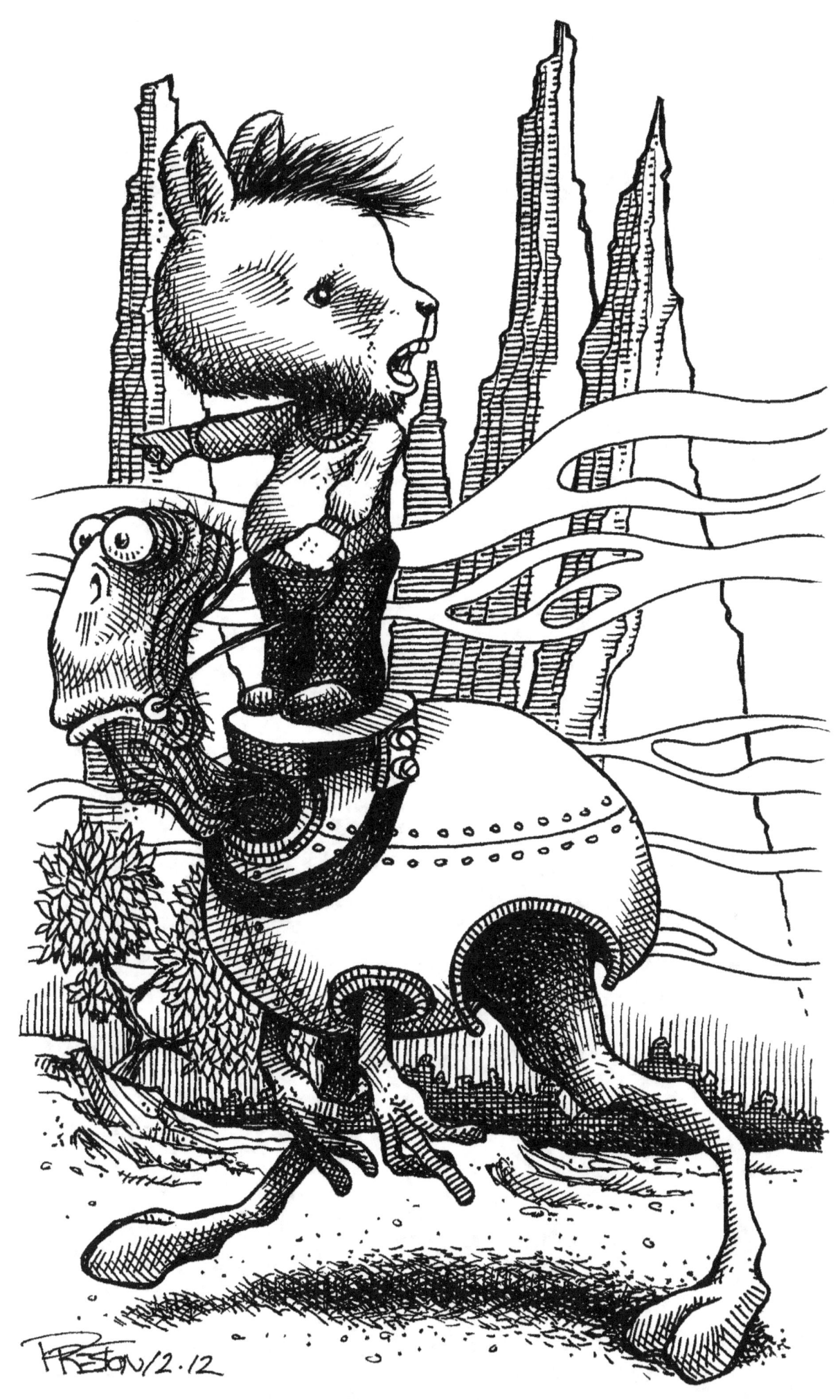

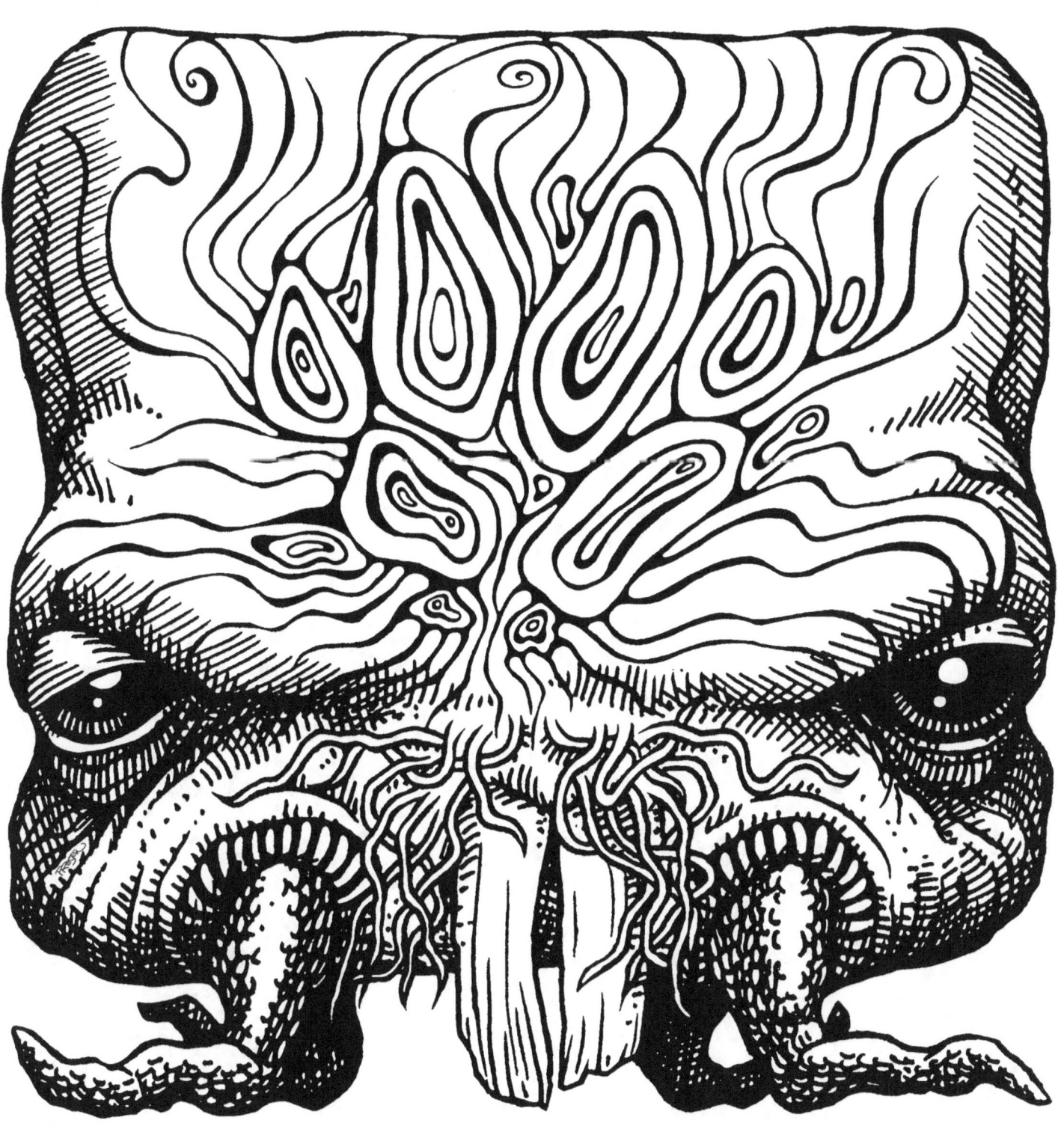

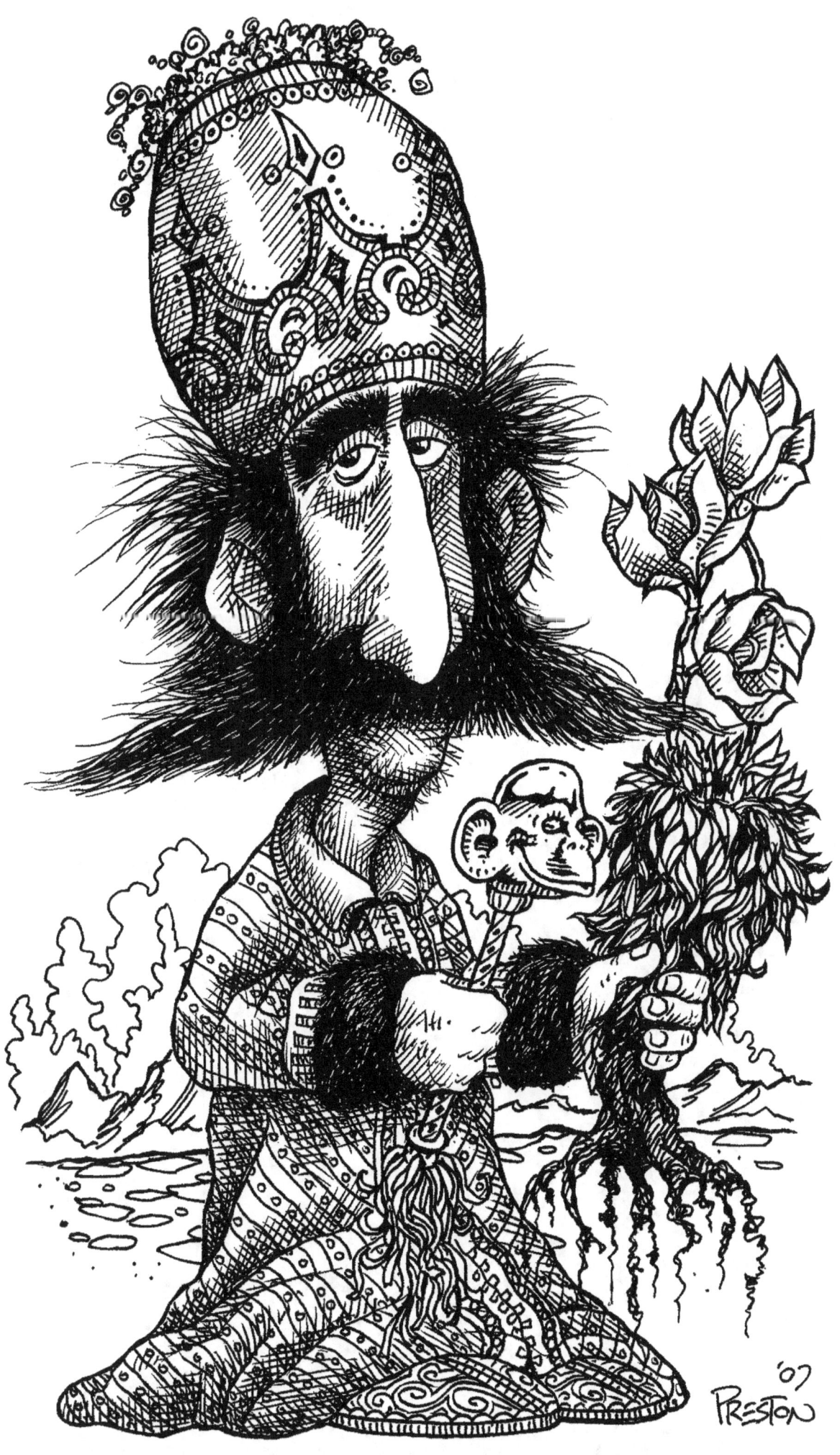

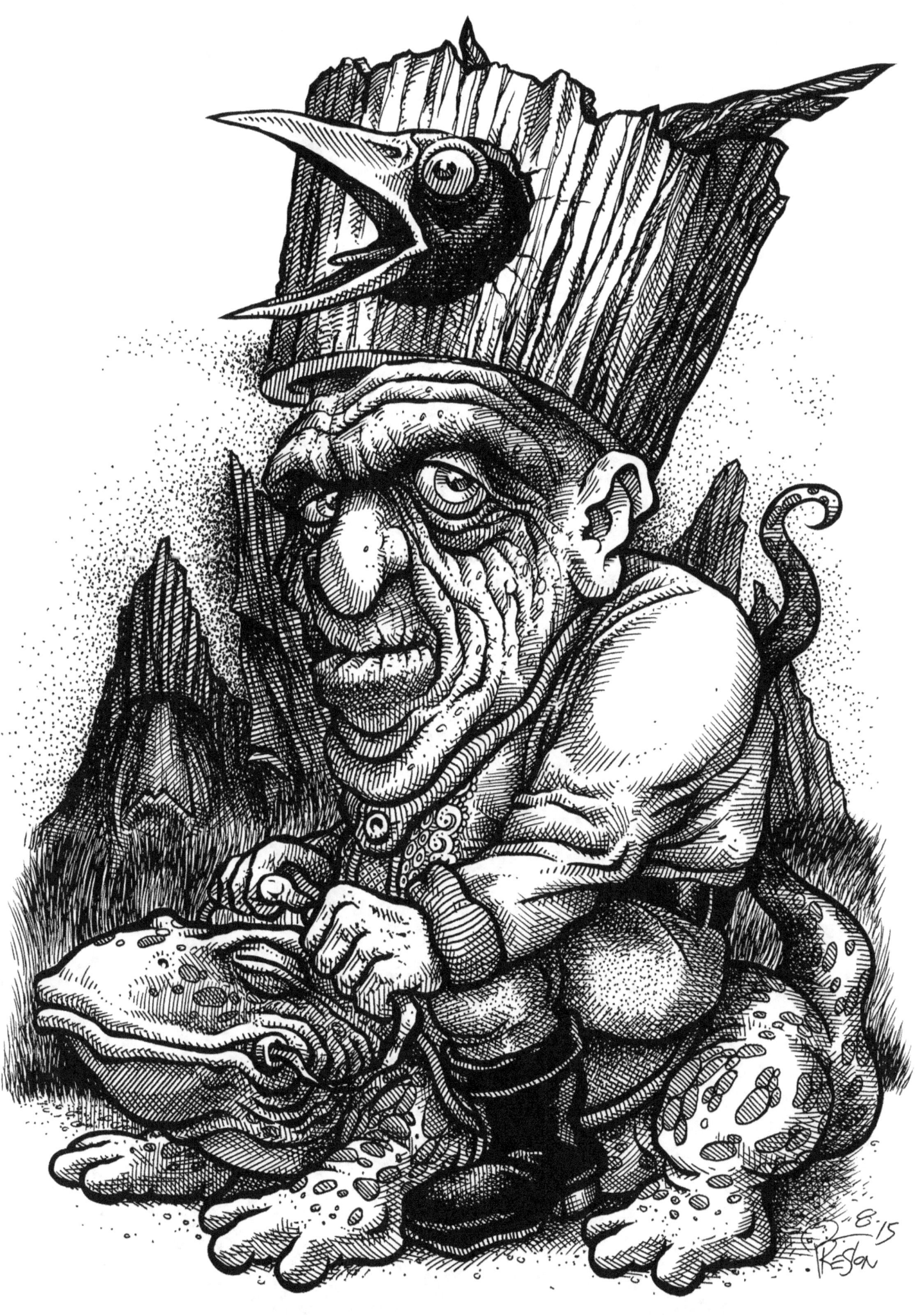

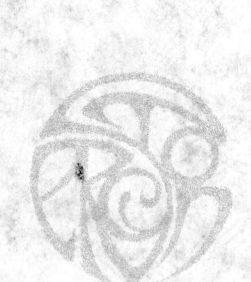

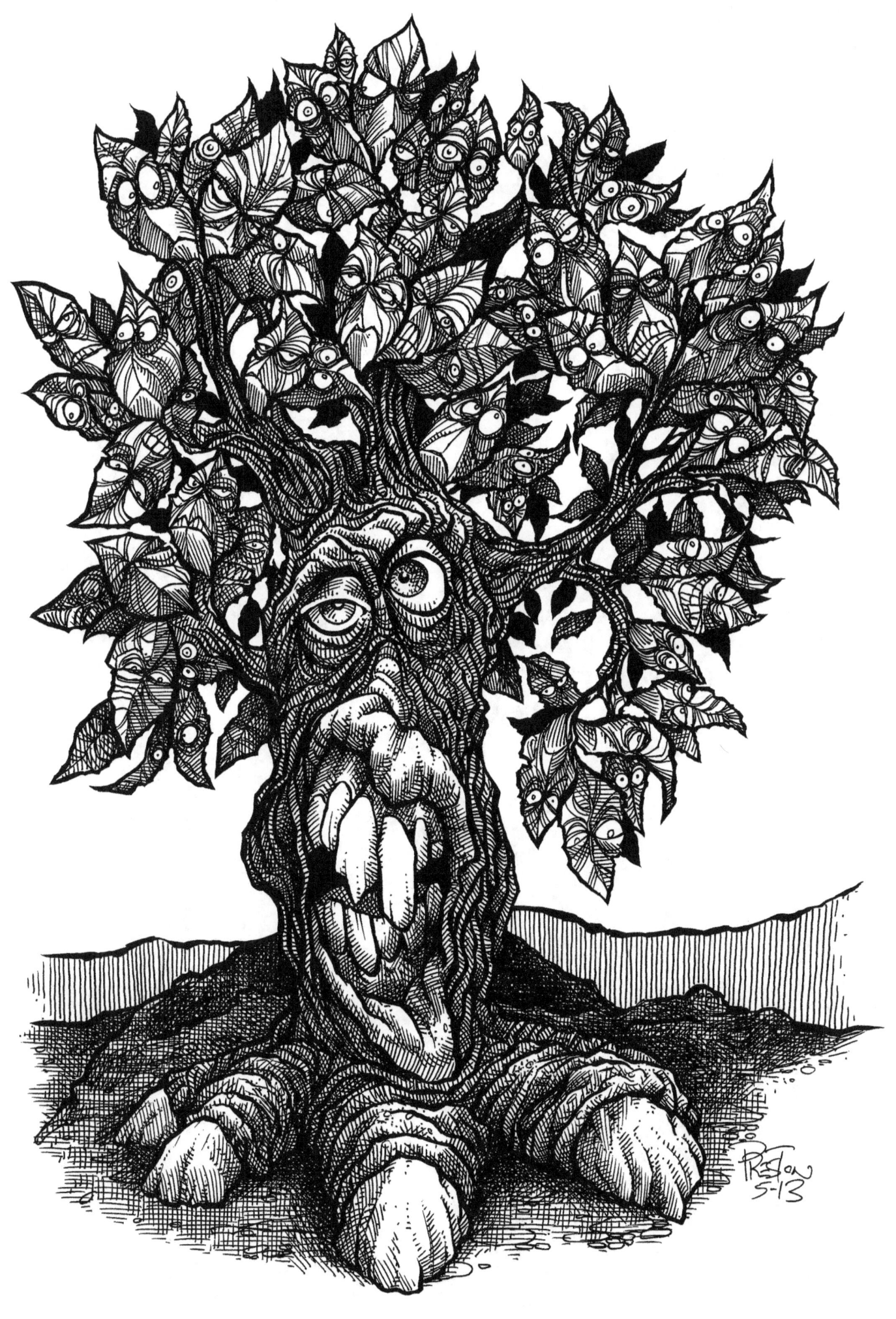

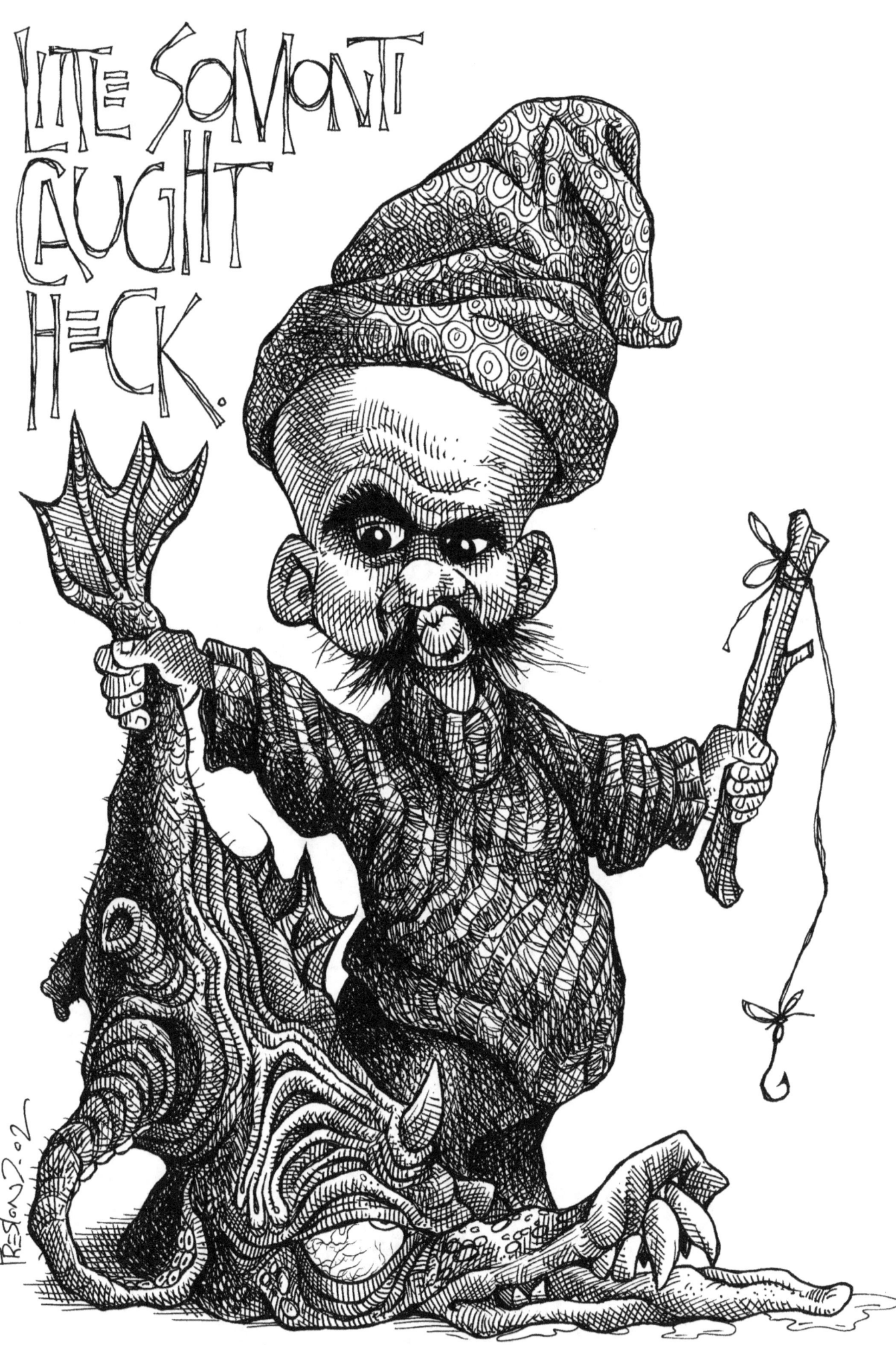

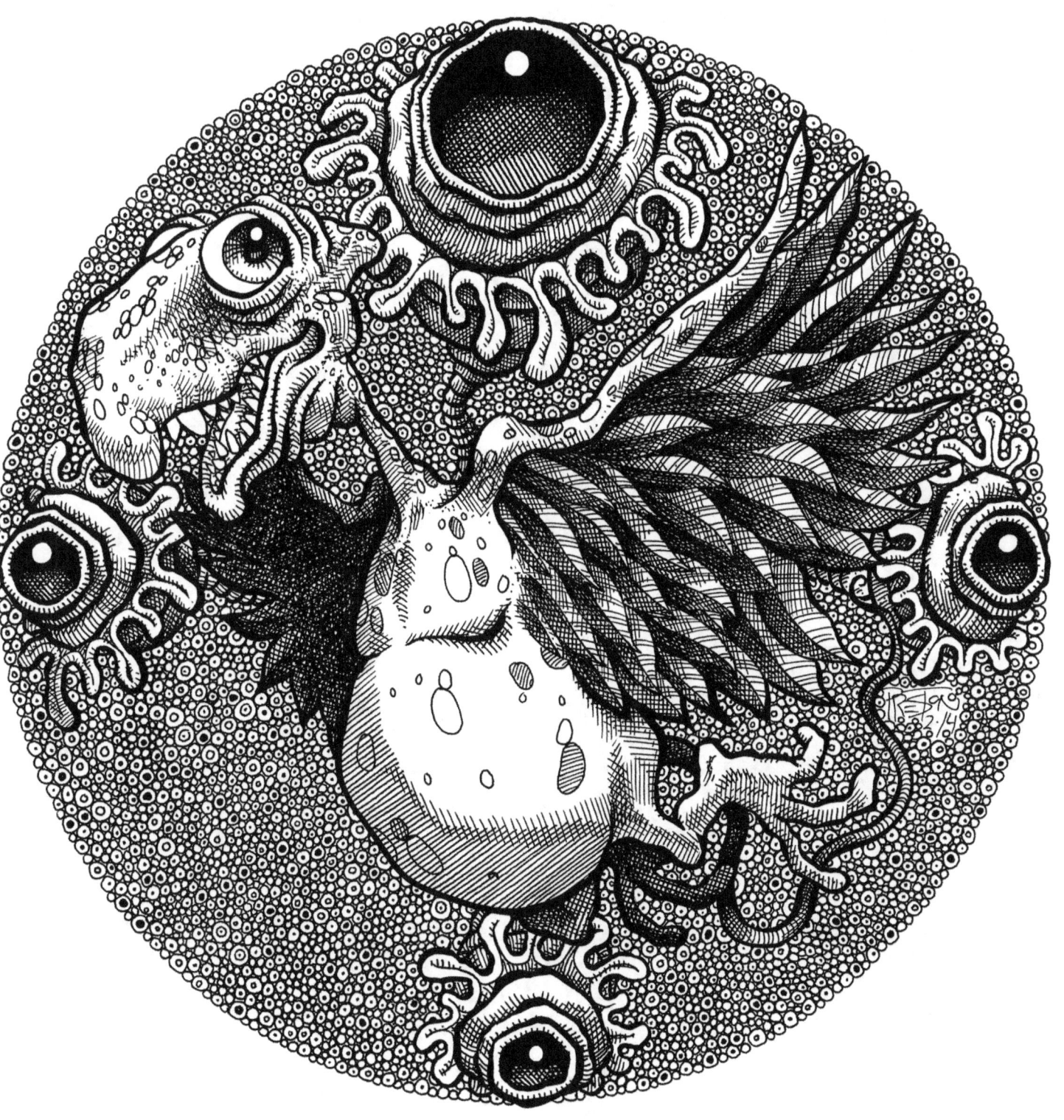

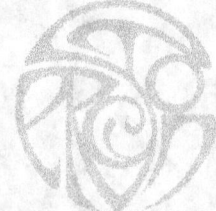

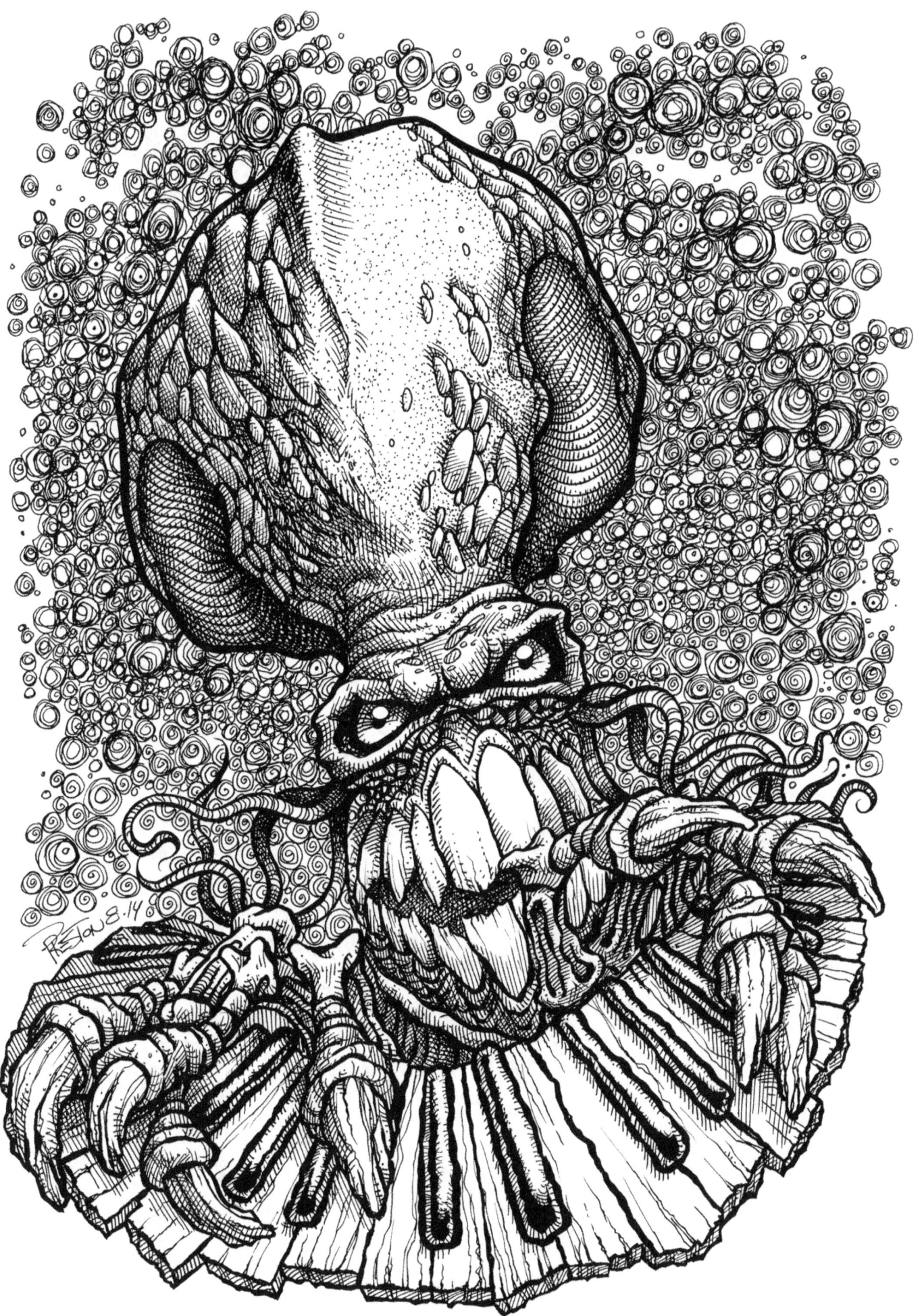

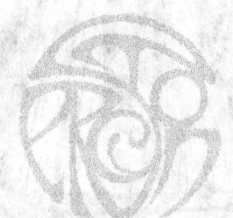

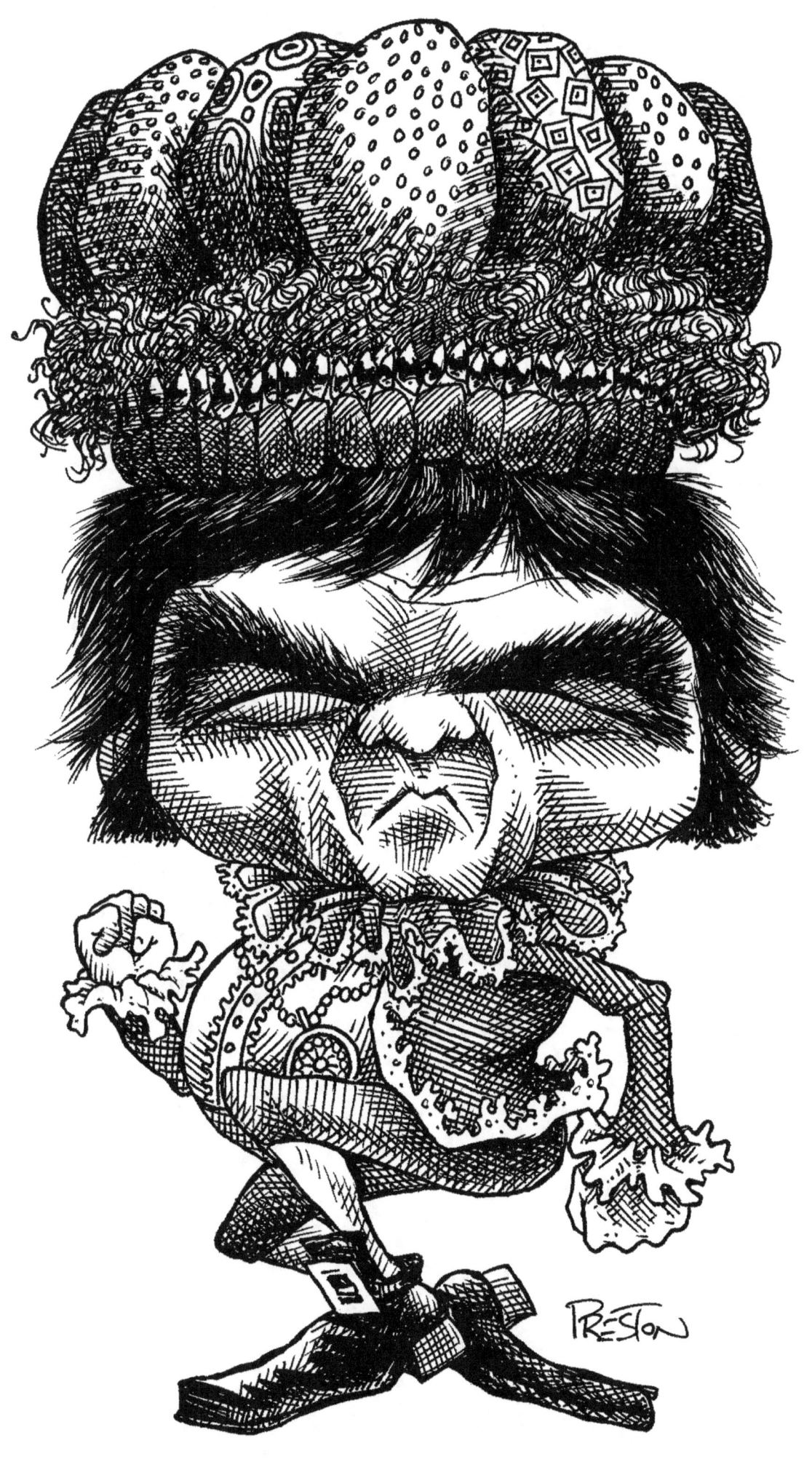

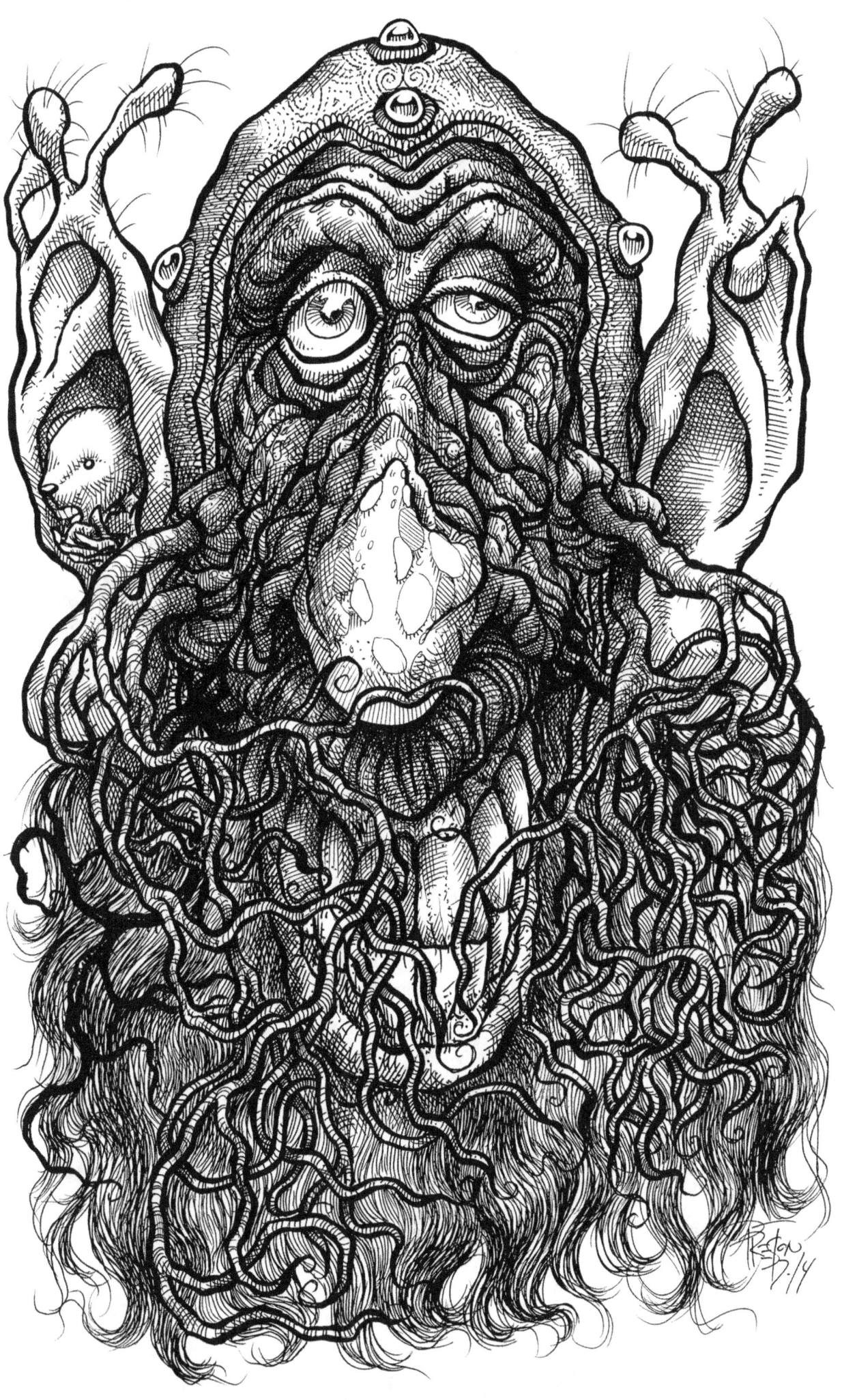

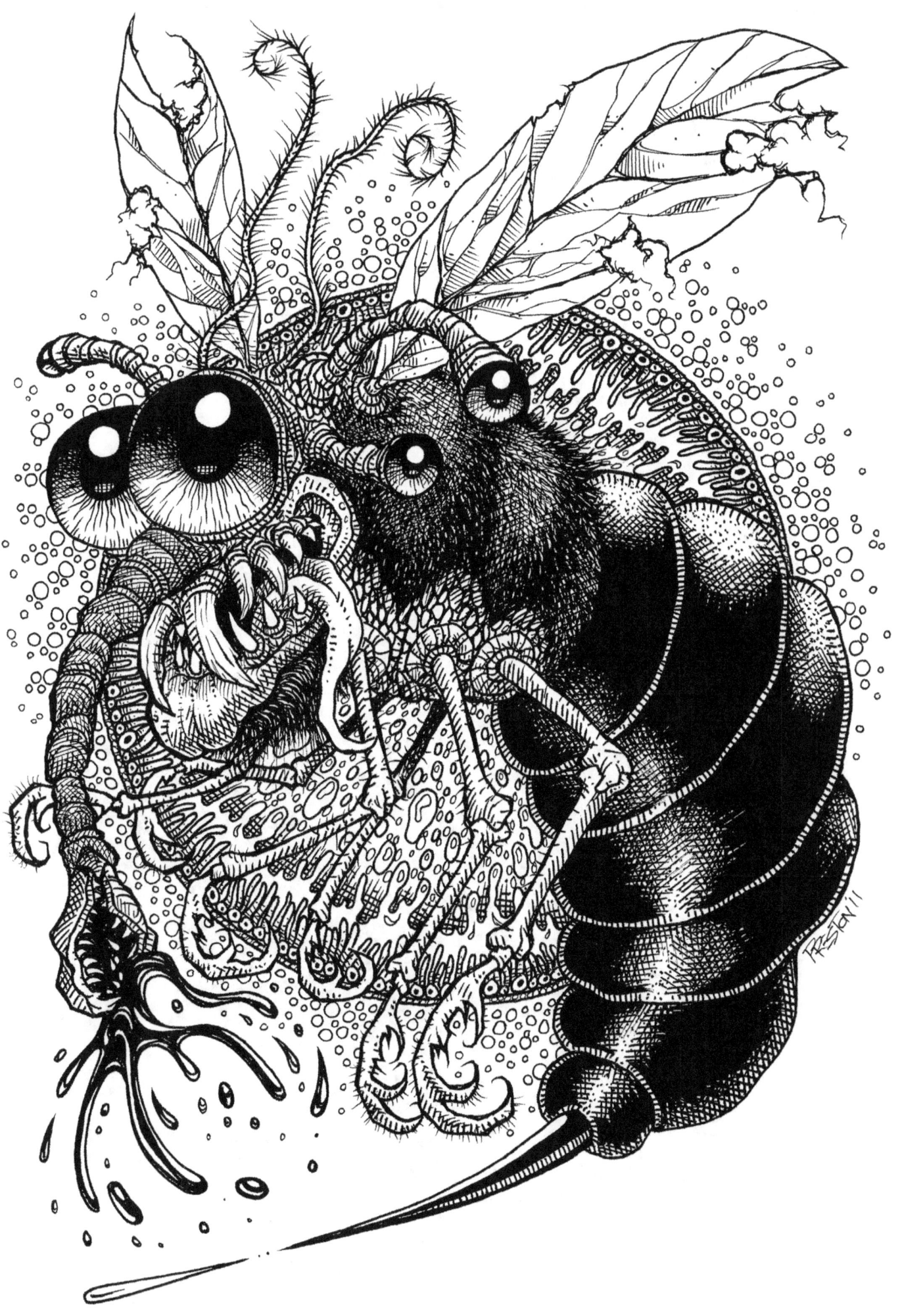

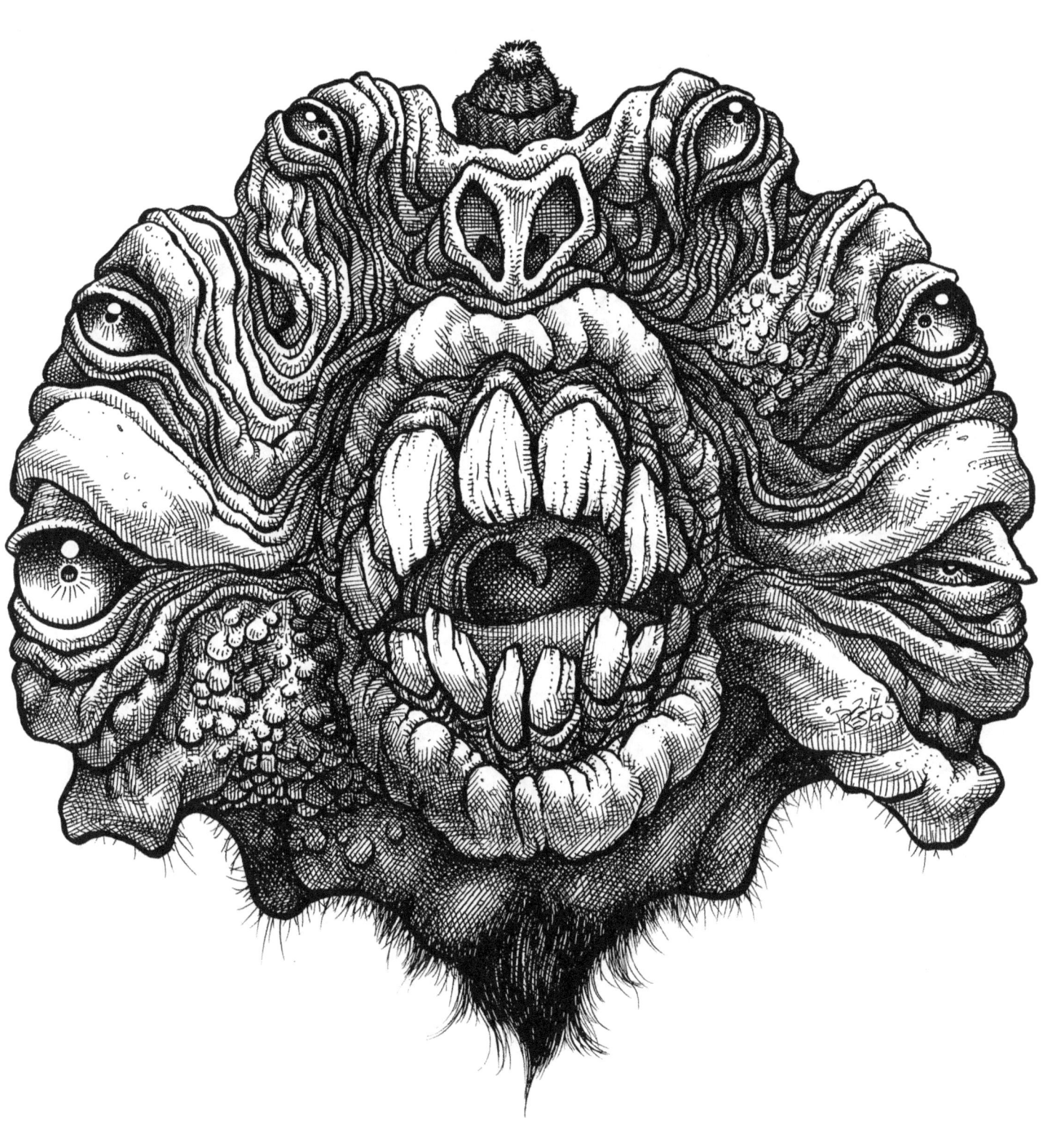

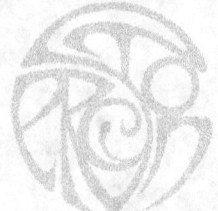

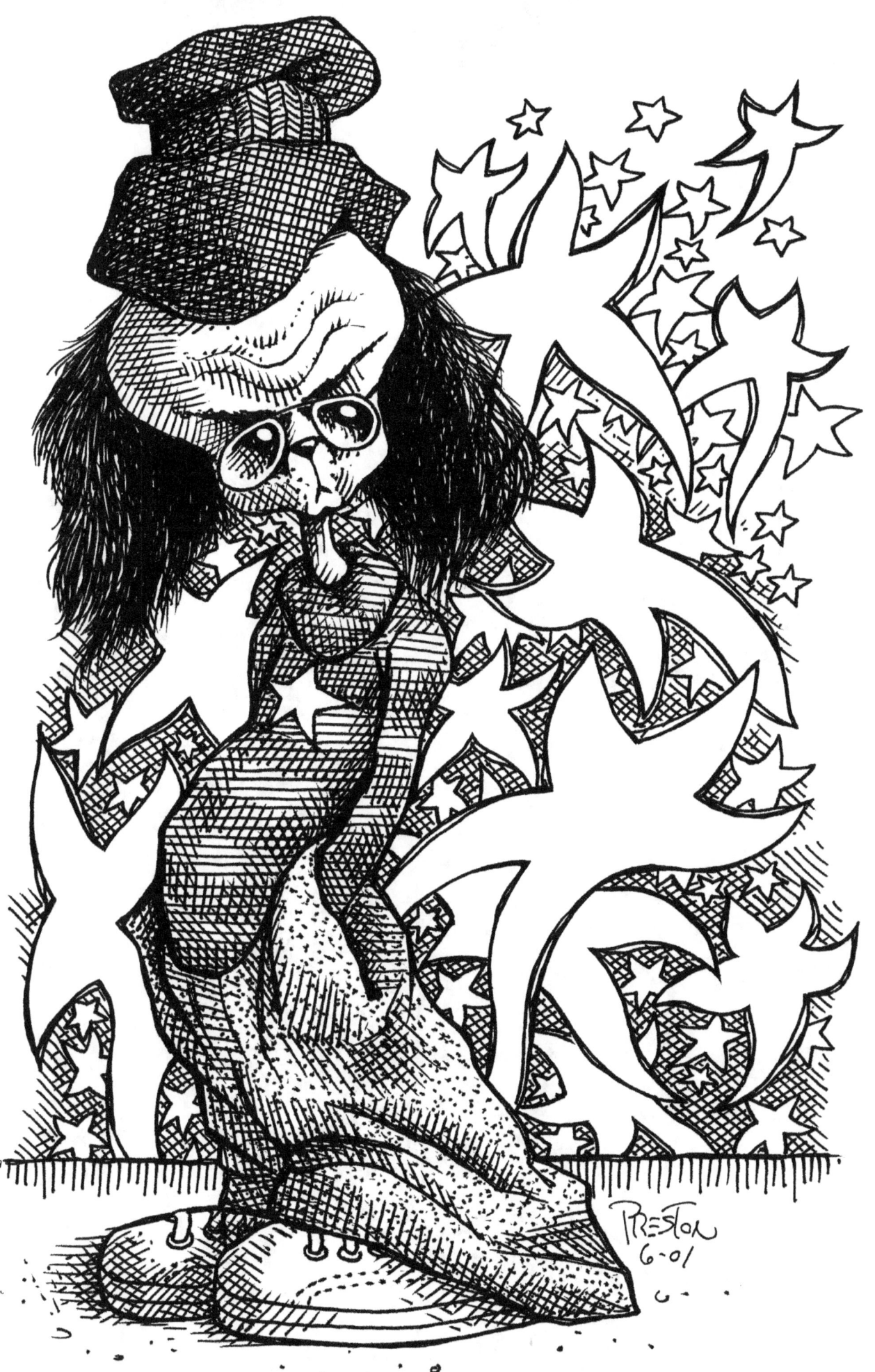

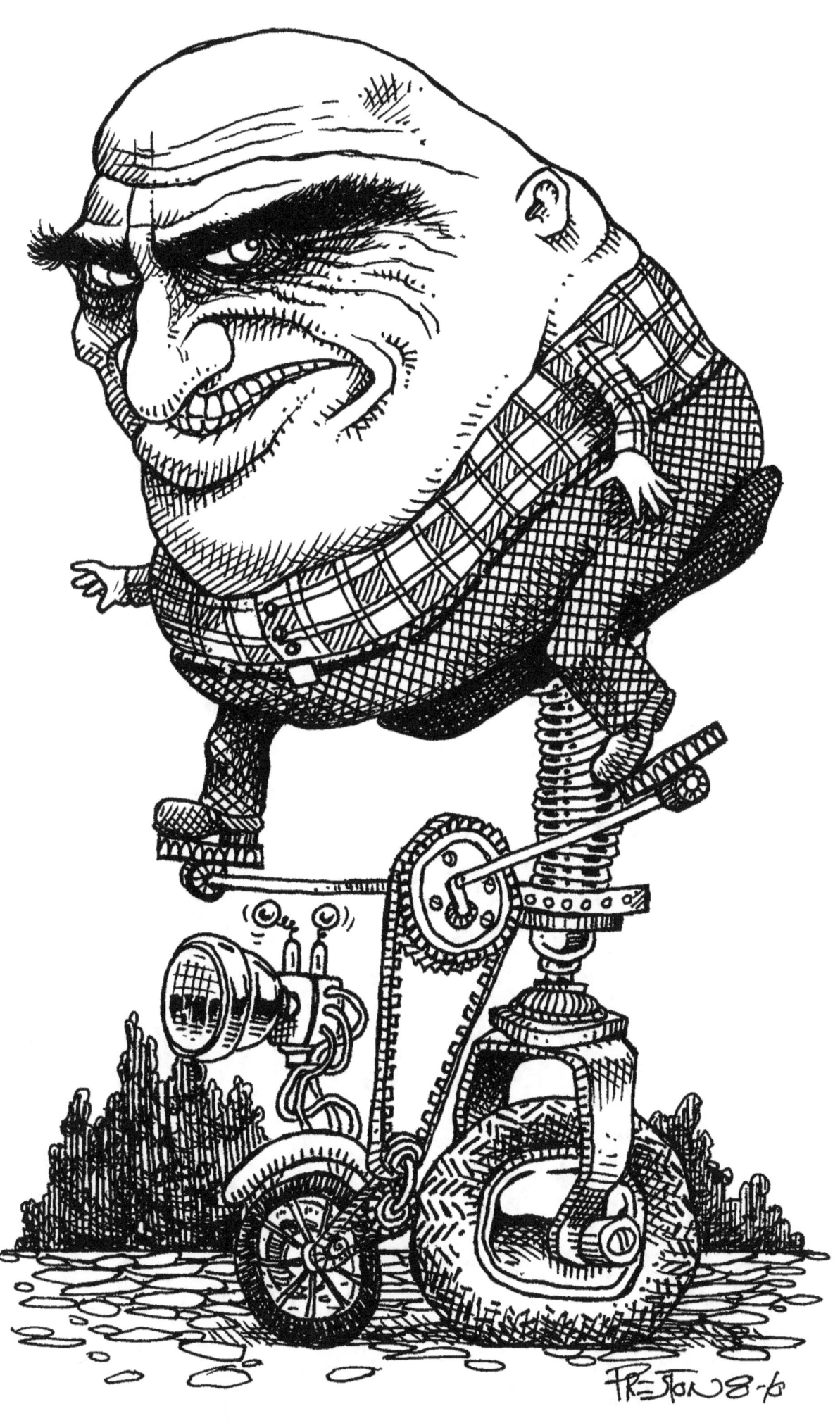

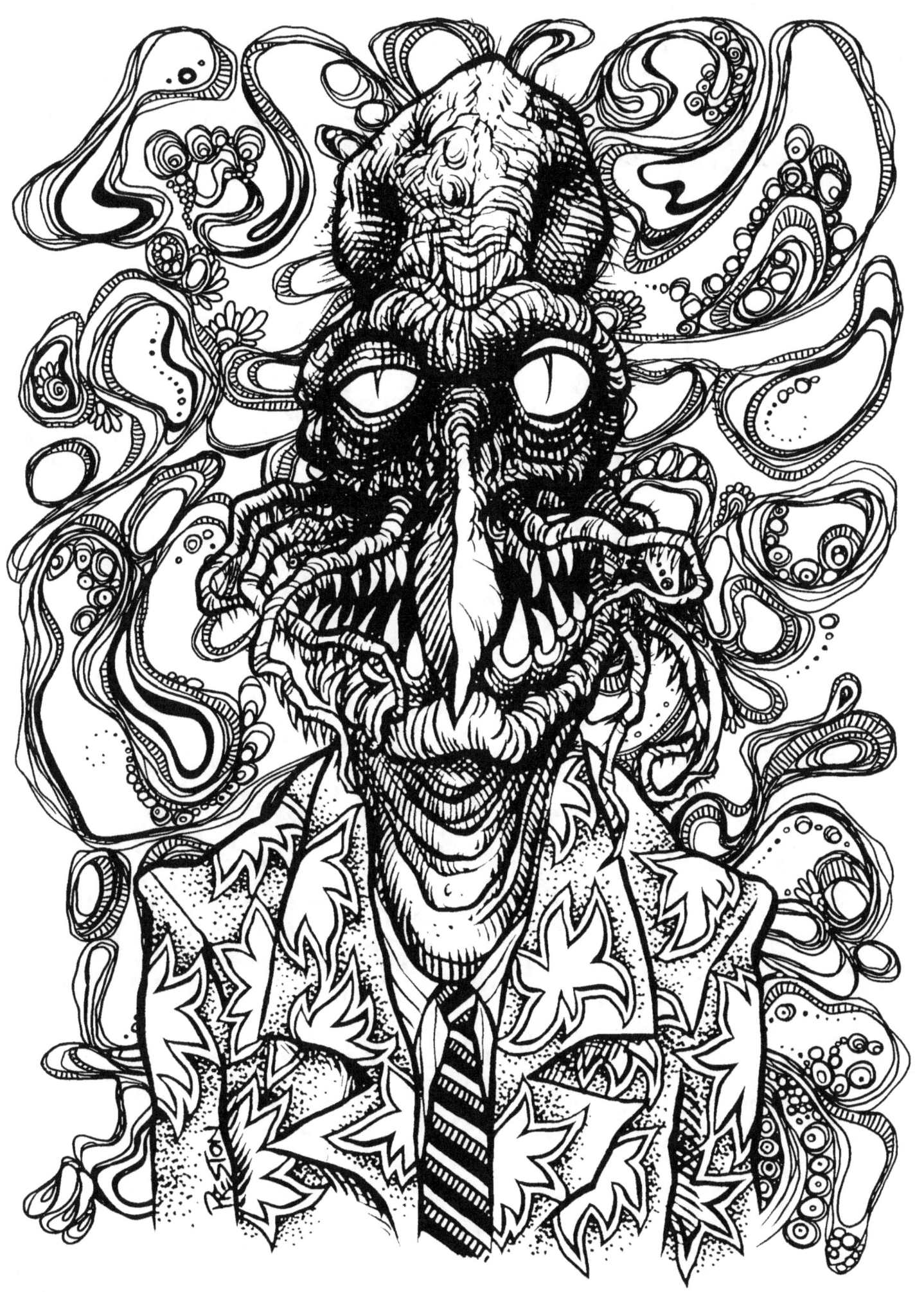

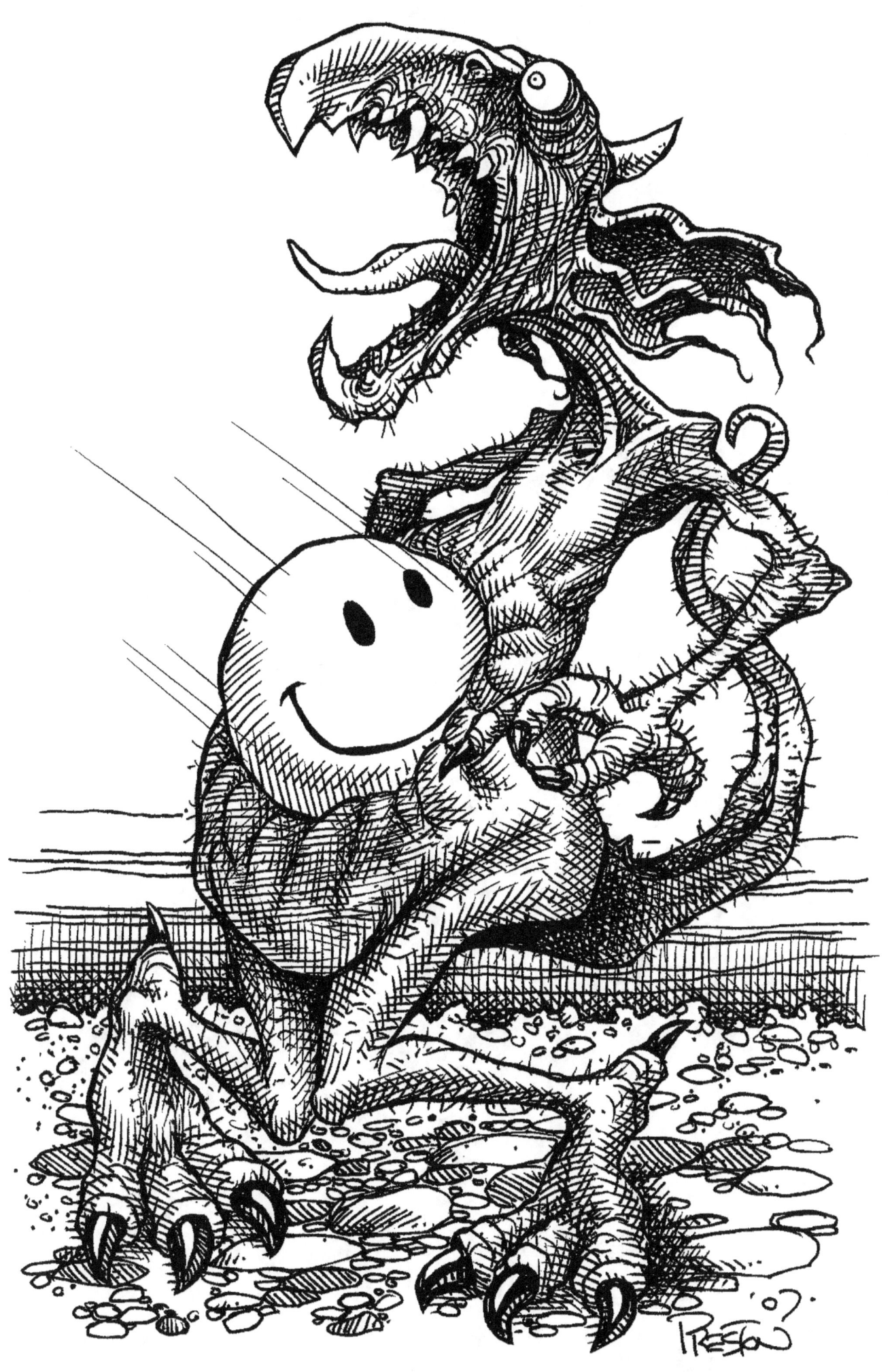

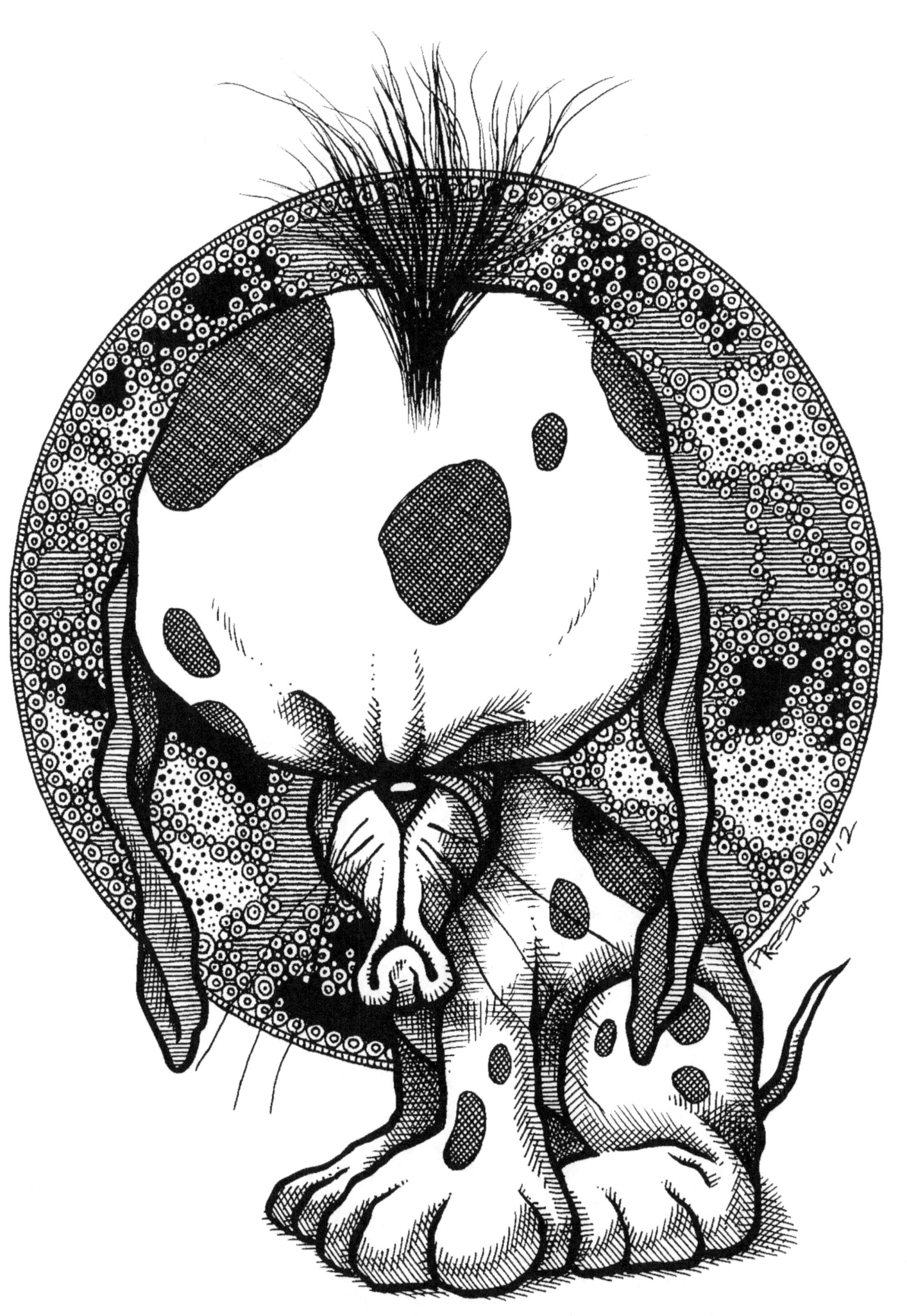

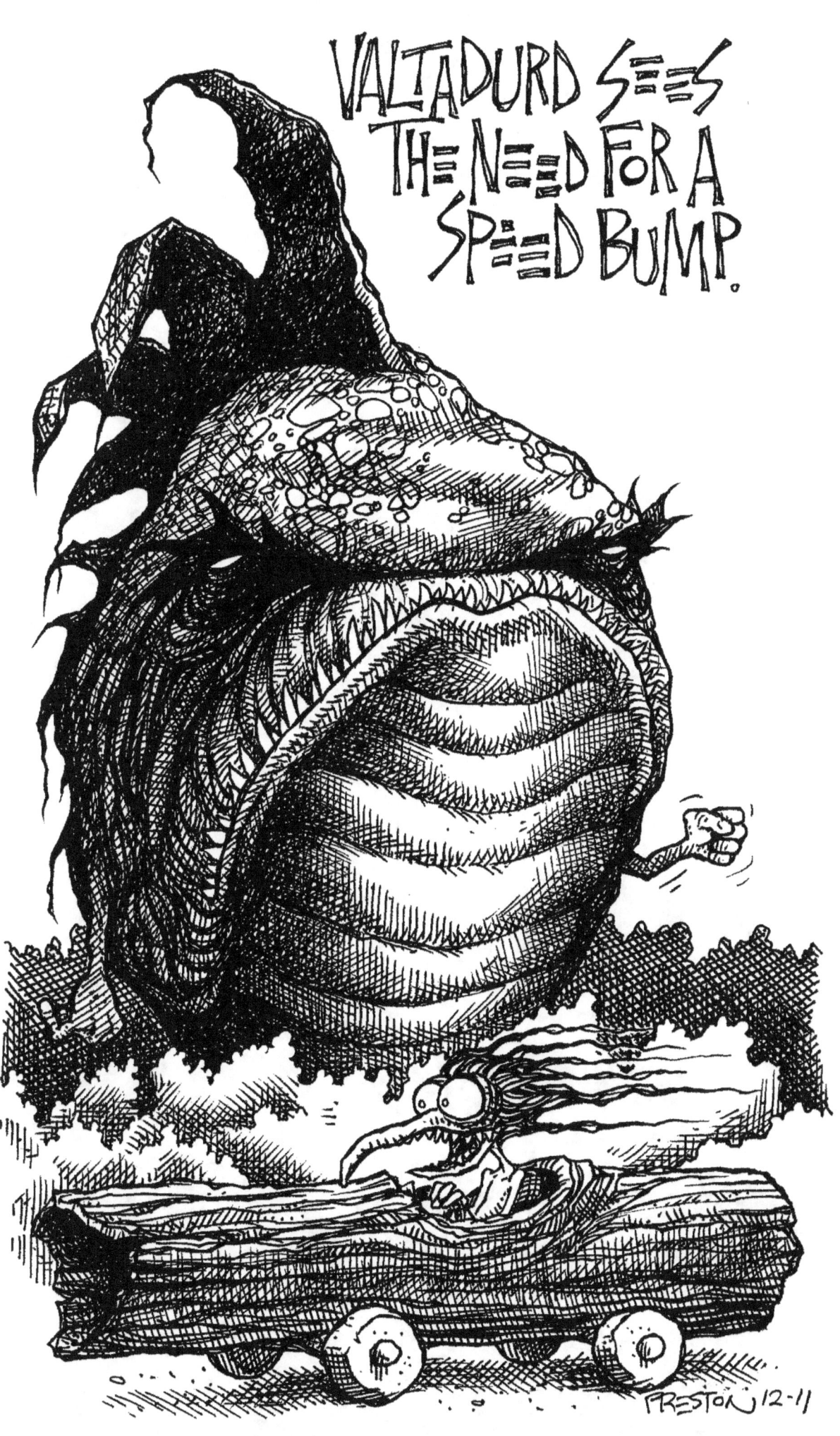

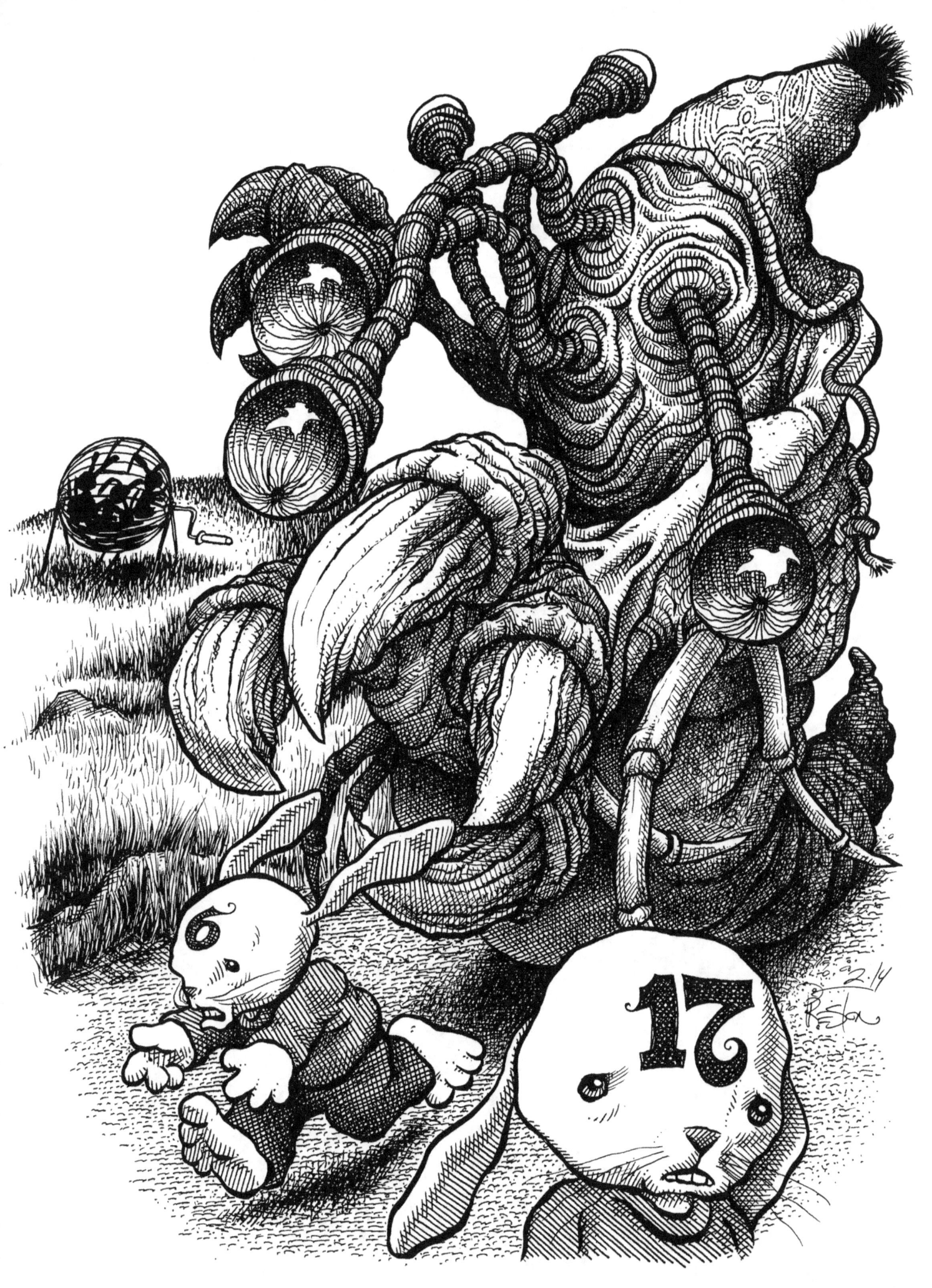

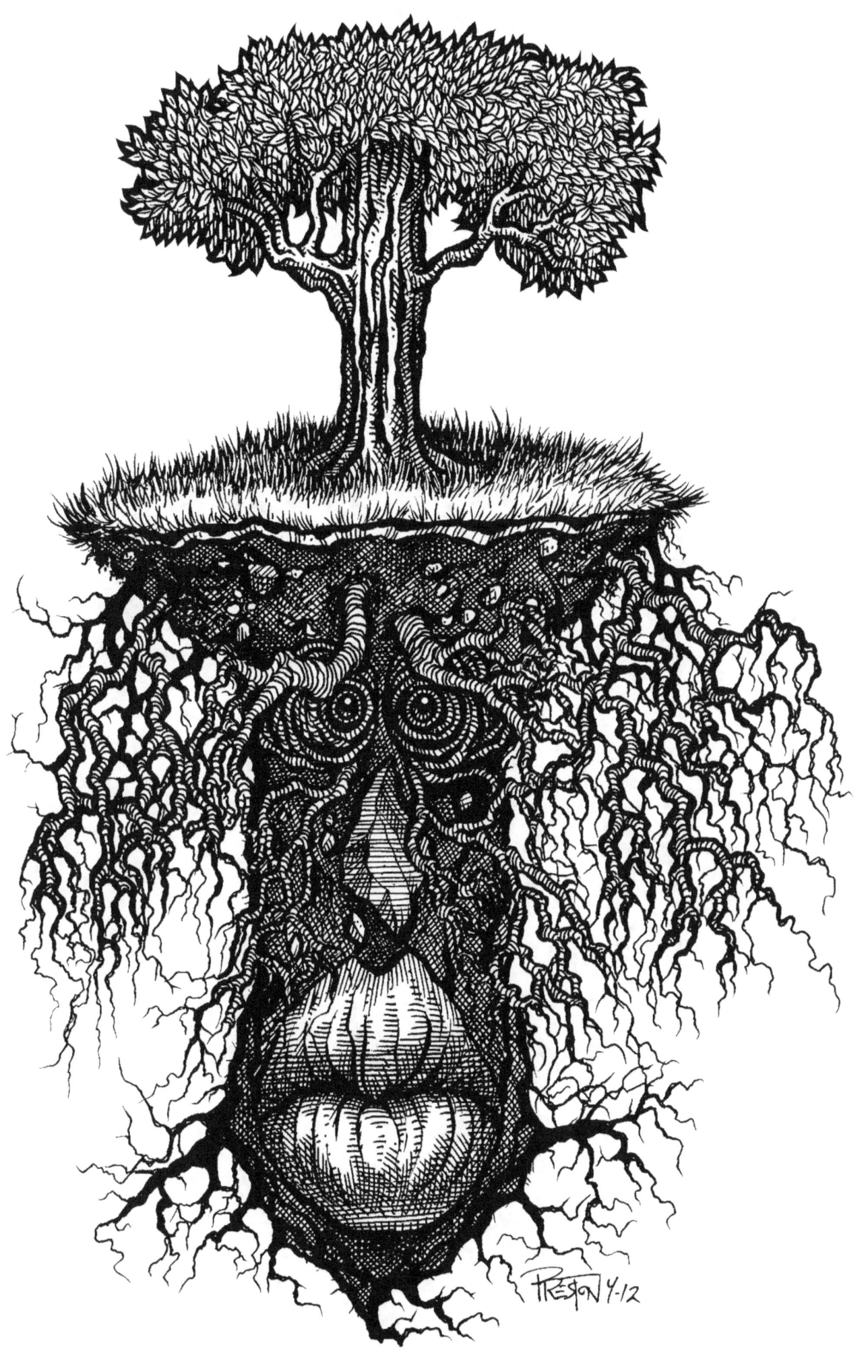

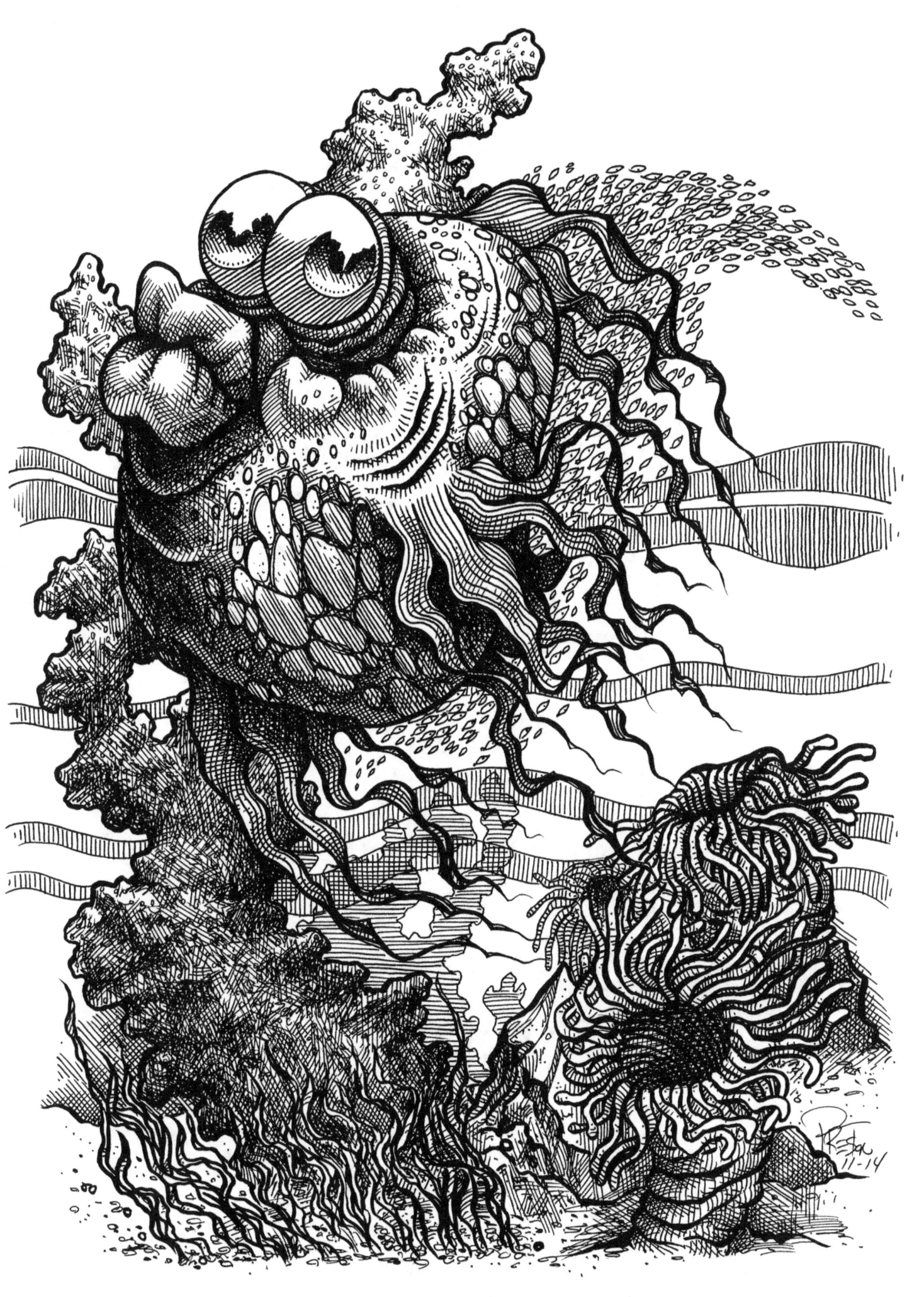

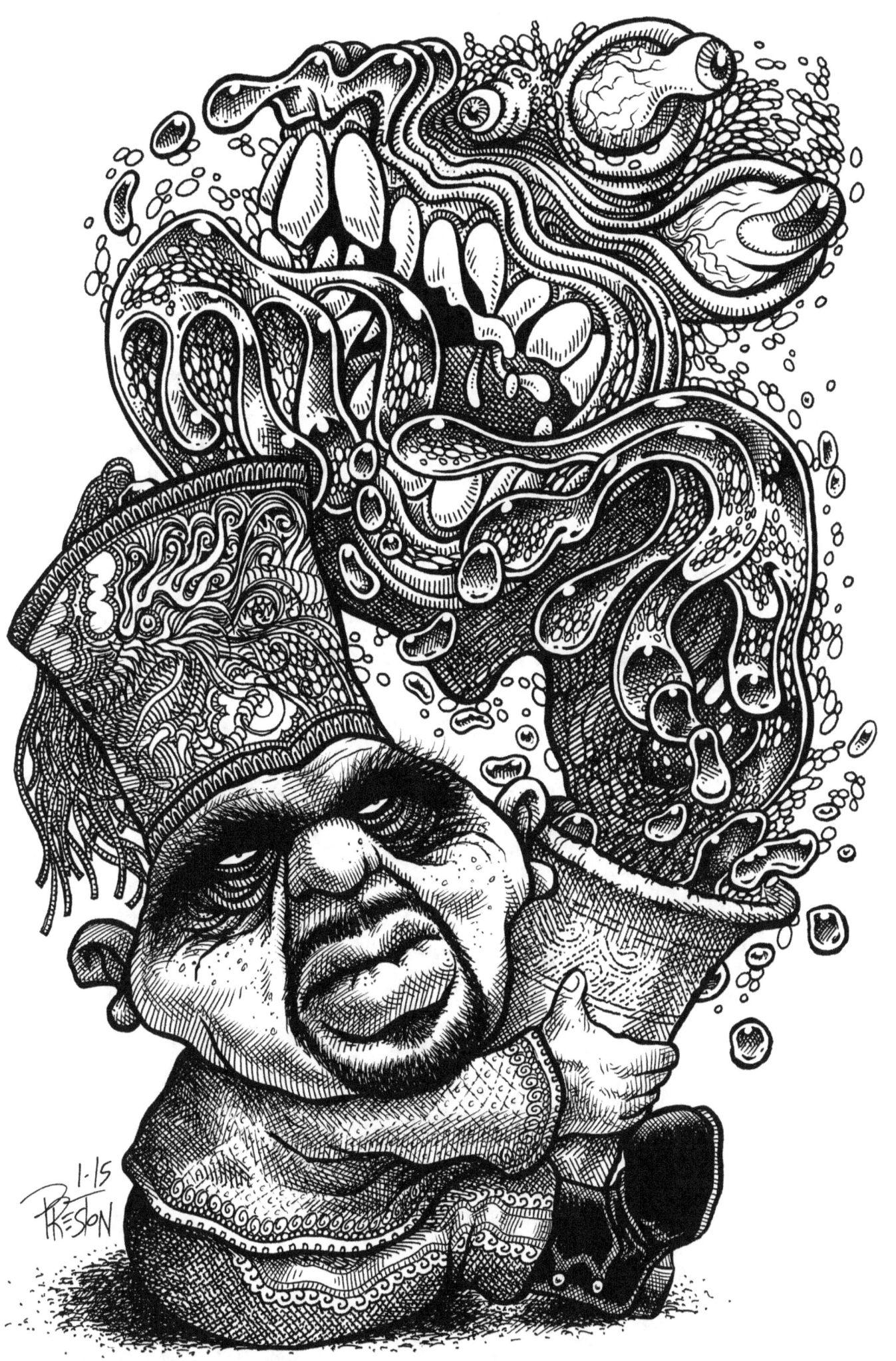

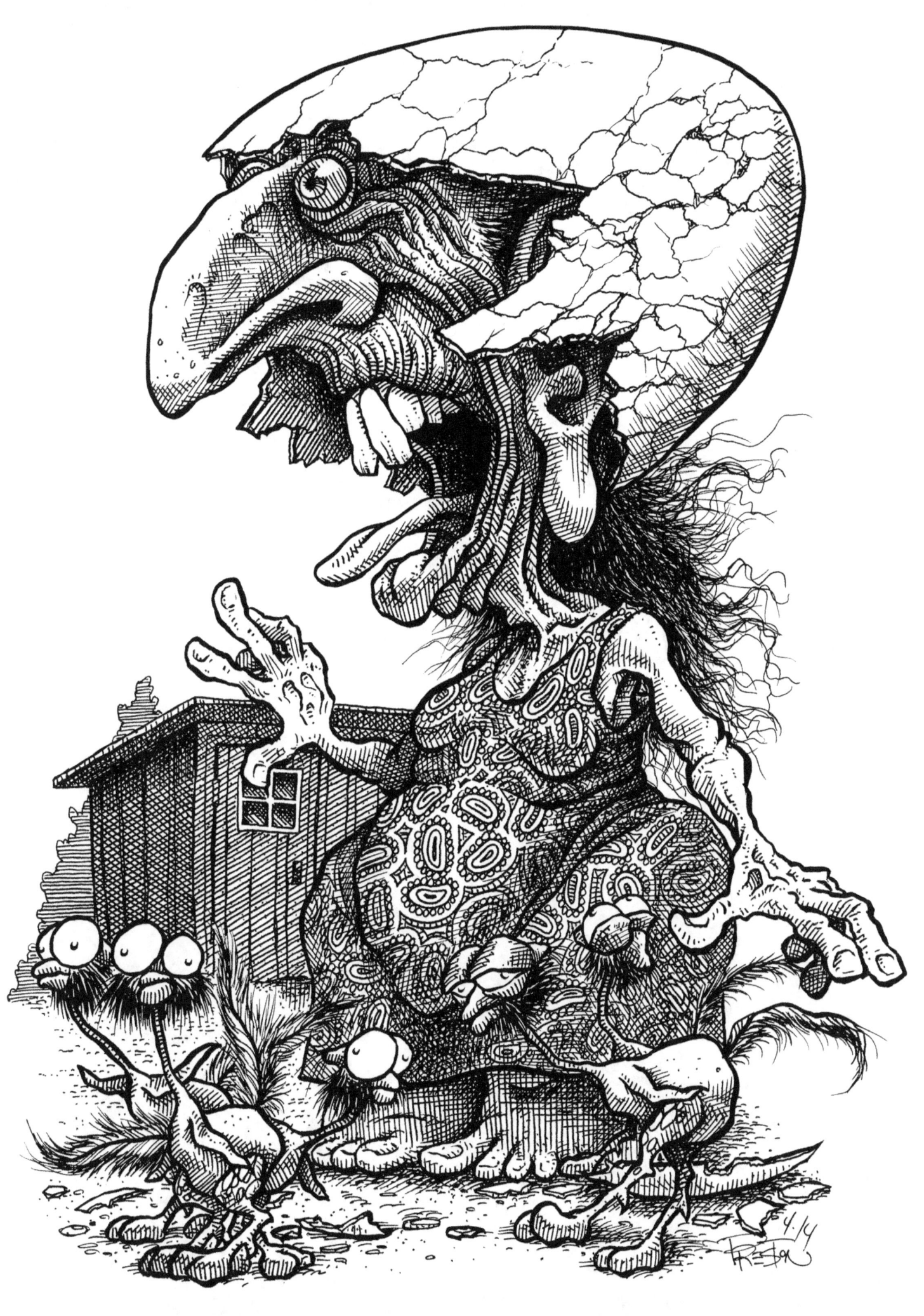

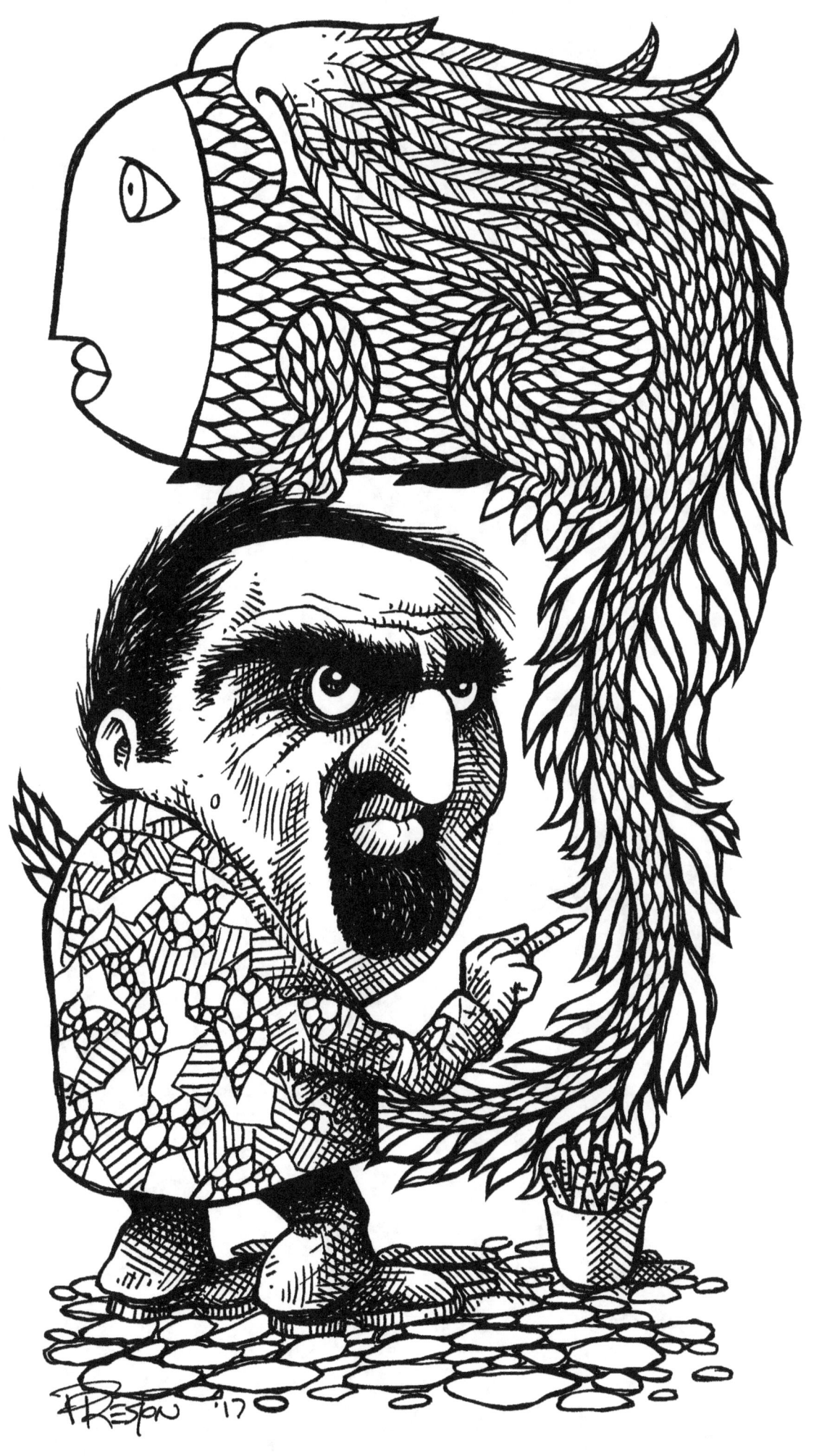

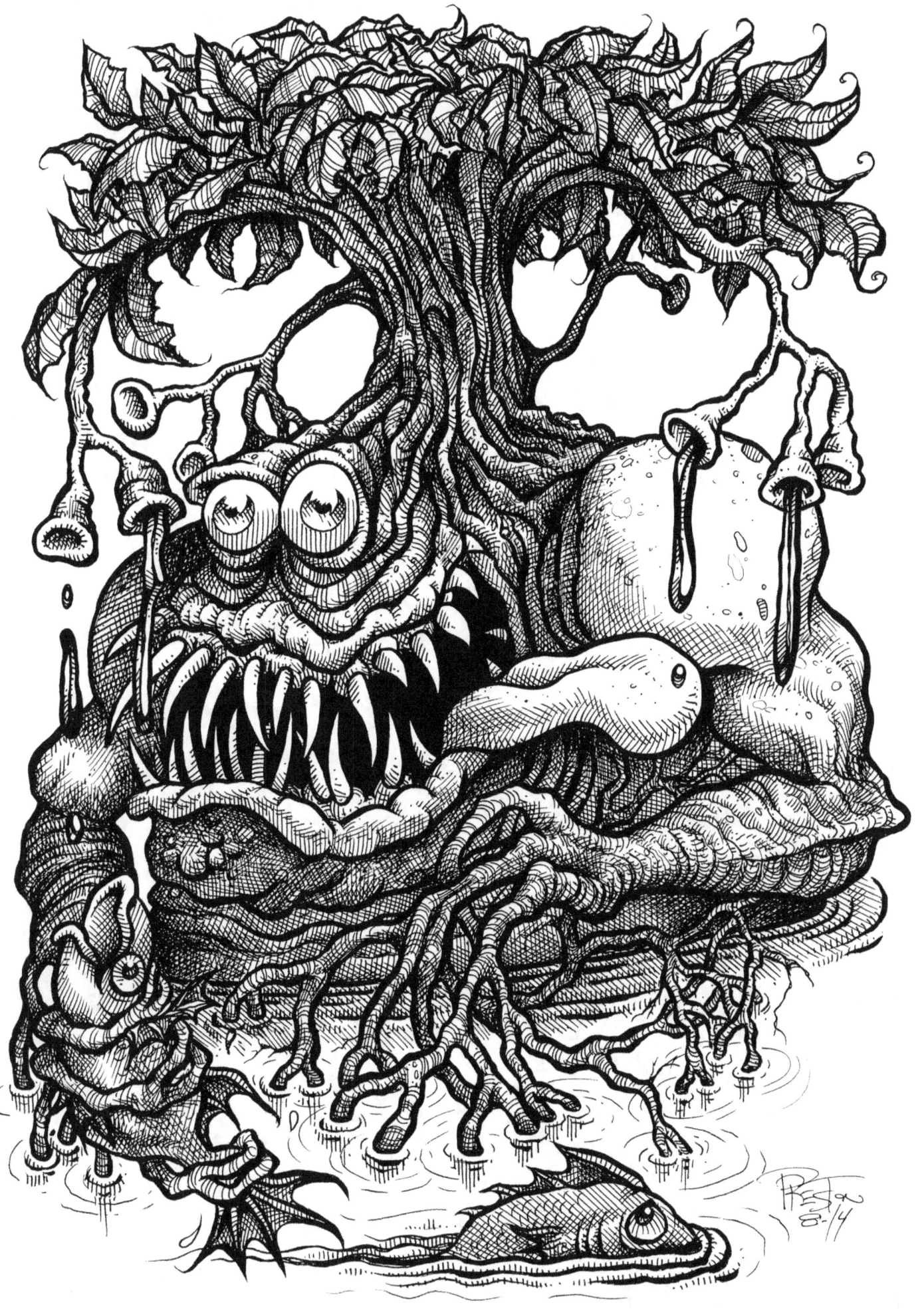

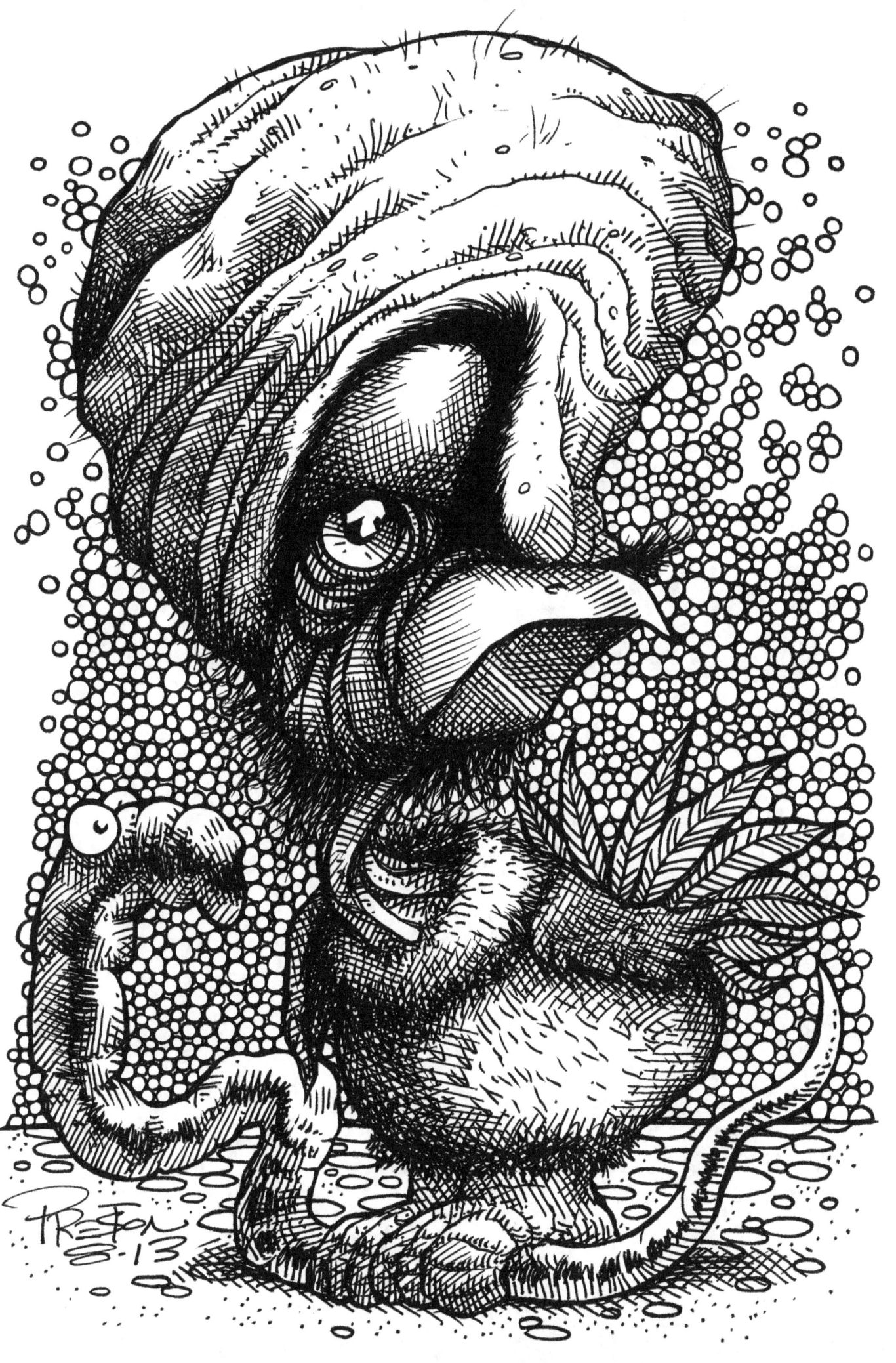

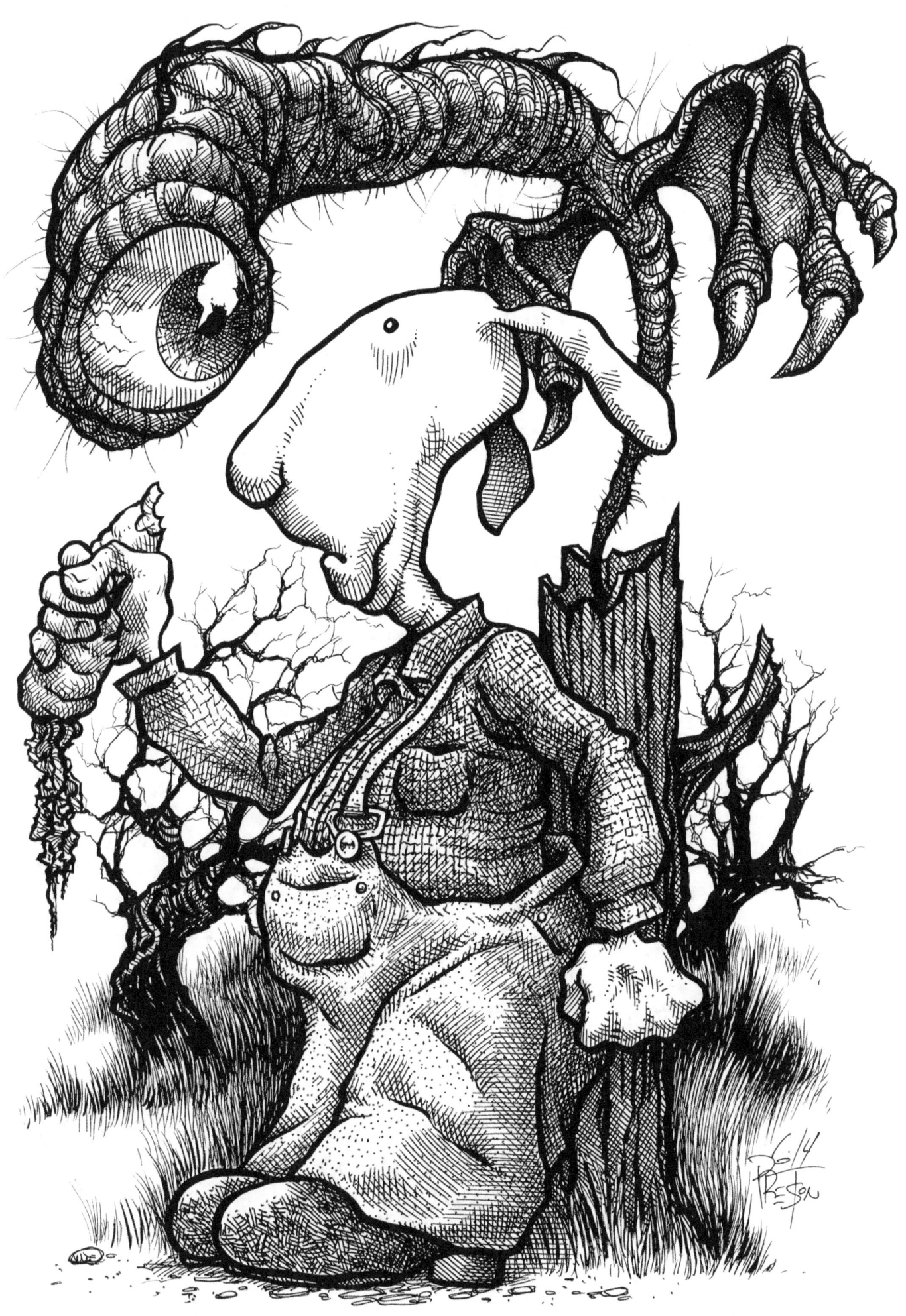

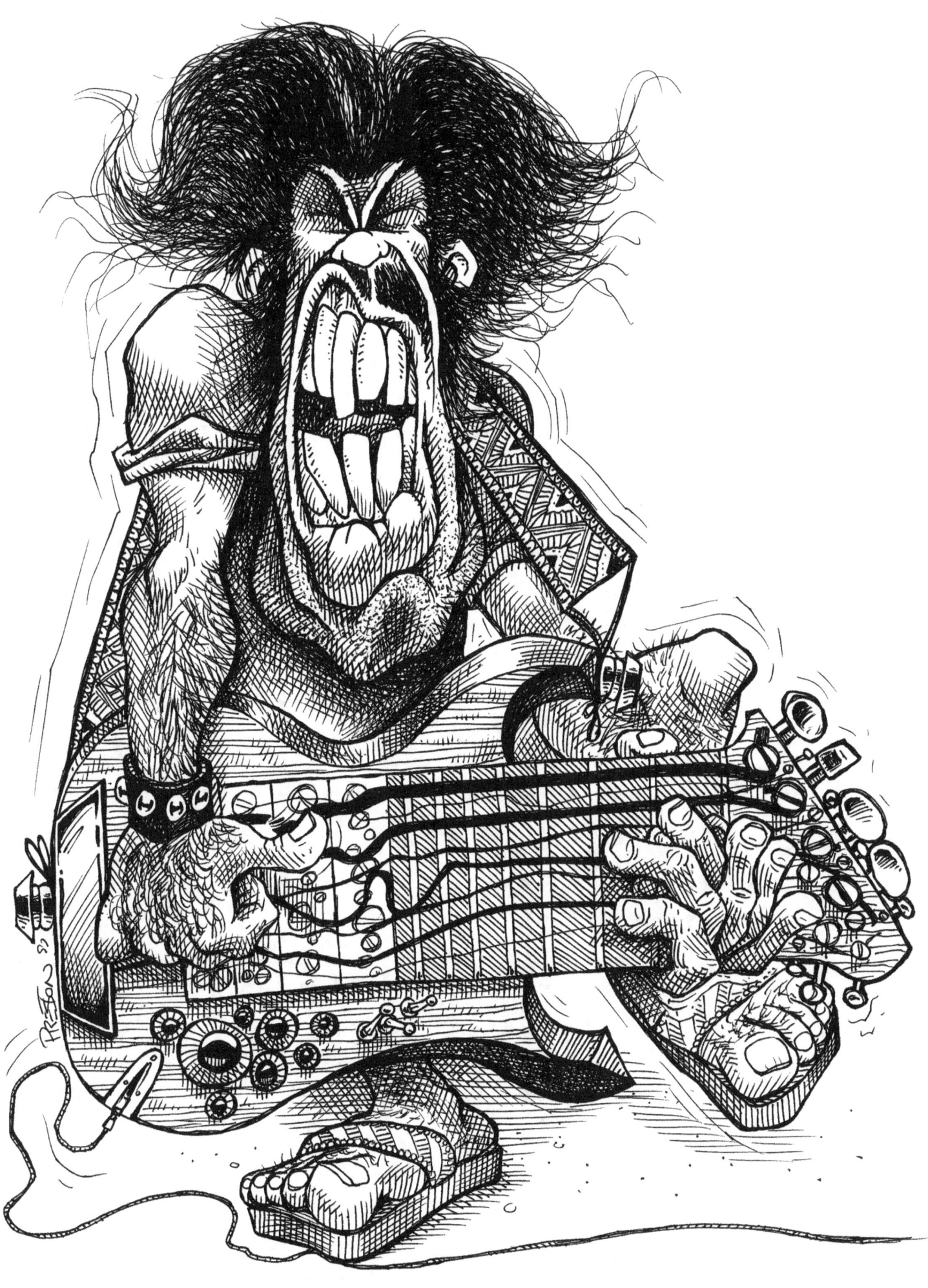

SHAUN HAS AN UGLY THOUGHT.

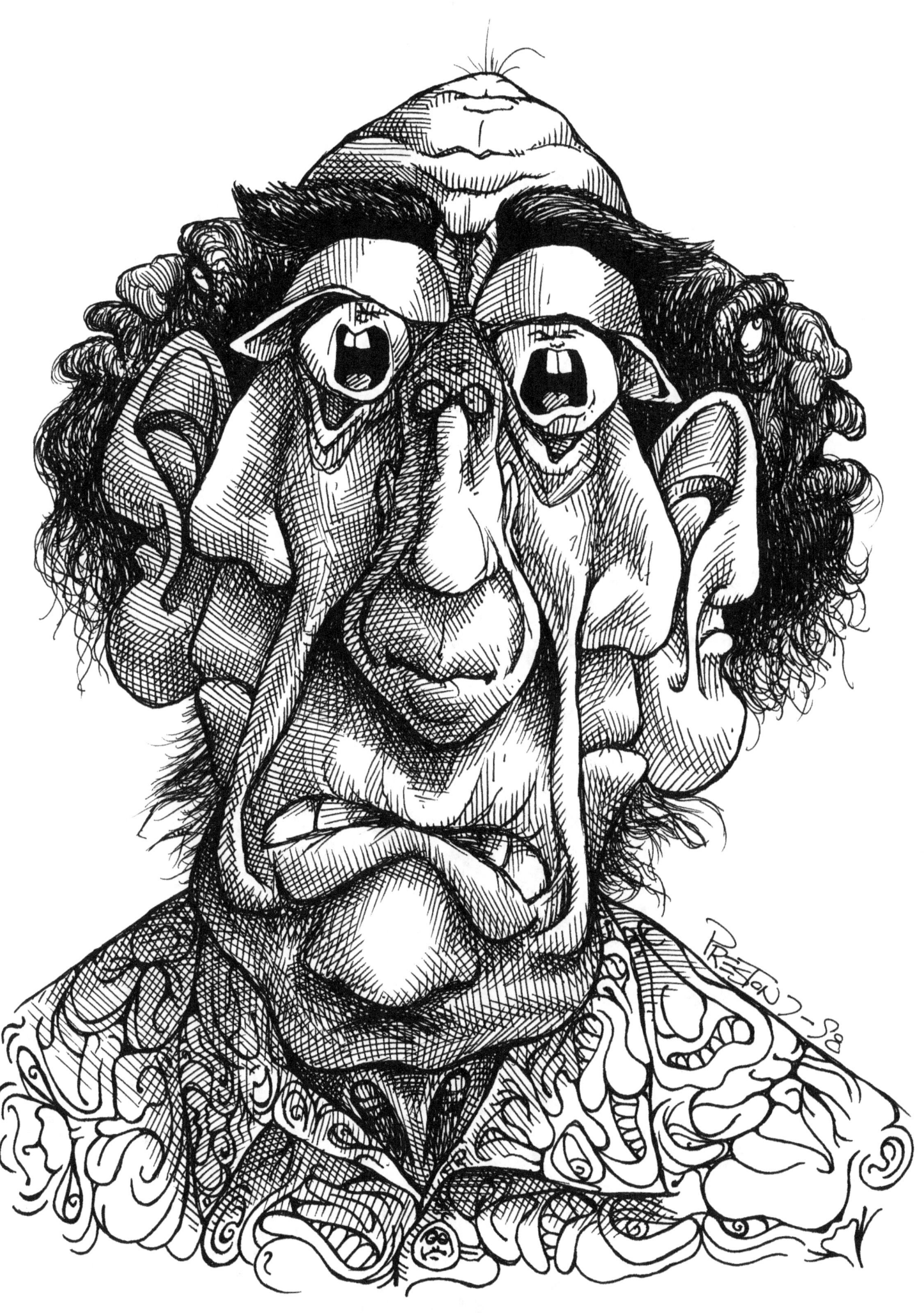

www.ingramcontent.com/pod-product-compliance
Lightning Source LLC
Chambersburg PA
CBHW081216170526
45165CB00009B/2841